# Contents

# 1 INTO ITALY

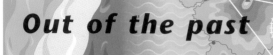
▶ How does Italy's history affect its geography?
▶ How is Italy divided for administration?
▶ What links does Italy have with other European countries?

### The Roman influence

Italy's geography owes much to its history. Between about 100BC and AD400, the Roman Empire stretched from Britain to present-day Turkey and from Germany to North Africa. Some effects of Roman rule can still be seen in the landscapes both of Italy and of other European countries. There are remains of Roman buildings, as well as the sites and grid-pattern street layouts of Roman towns and cities. Many modern roads follow roads that were built by the Romans. People's language, culture and the course of European history have been affected by the Ancient Romans.

### Middle Ages Italy

In the Middle Ages, the main cities in Italy were run as independent countries called **city states**. The cities such as Venice, Florence and Genoa grew rich because of their industries, commerce and trade. Much of Italy's architecture and art treasures come from the **Renaissance** period between about 1200 and 1600. Today, millions of visitors come to Italy to see these cities and works of art.

Italy did not become a united country until 1871. Even then, the Vatican City and San Marino did not agree to join. Now they are both independent countries inside Italy. So unlike many other European countries, the modern country of Italy has a quite recent history. This is one reason why Italians often see themselves first as from their city or region, and secondly as Italian. This can be a problem when the government tries to use taxes to help the country's poorer regions.

### Administrative regions

Italy has a president, a prime minister and a national parliament. There is no **monarchy** in Italy so the country is called a **republic**. The country is divided into 20 **administrative regions**. These are large areas that have their

**A** The Spanish Steps in Rome

4

**B The administrative regions of Italy**

Key
— · — International boundary
------- Regional boundary

own regional president and elected councils. Each region makes some of its own laws and collects its own taxes. Each region is divided into several smaller areas called **provinces**.

Statistics for Italy's population and **economy** are collected for the administrative regions and provinces. There are often great differences in people's standard of living and in the economy between the regions. There are also great differences between the provinces within each region. One aim of the Italian government is to reduce these differences.

## The European connection

In 1956, Italy was one of the six countries that came together to form the European Economic Community (EEC). This was done when the Treaty of Rome was signed. The EEC is now named the **European Union** (EU), with fifteen member countries.

Agreements between EU countries mean that Italy can **trade** without paying import and export taxes to other EU countries. This has helped Italy to become a modern industrial country. The EU has also helped some of the poorer regions in Italy with grants of money. The money helps support peasant farmers. It also encourages industry to locate in areas with the greatest economic and social problems.

**C The port of Salerno in south-west Italy**

## FACT FILE

### Language in Italy
Italy takes its name from a Latin word that means grazing, or where there were oxen. The Latin language is now a dead language that no one speaks. However, many Latin words have become part of English, French and other languages.

Most people in Italy now speak Italian. This comes from a language that used to be spoken in Tuscany but which was changed by the Romans, who spoke Latin.

### Italian government
Italian people vote for politicians in their national parliament, which is called the Chamber of Deputies. There is also a Senate which, in some ways, is like the UK House of Lords. A difference is that Italian people vote for politicians in their Senate. The President is elected by politicians from the national and regional governments. The Prime Minister is appointed by the President. Italy had a king until 1945 when the country became a republic.

▶ **What is Italy's geography?**
▶ **How can we use maps to study places?**

## Using the land

Geography studies both people and nature at different scales, both large and small. These studies bring together ideas about:

- how the landscape is shaped by nature

- how and why people use land

- how natural processes and people interact to make each place unique, and show patterns that are similar

- questions and issues that people think about when they plan for the future.

The geography of a country studies how these ideas are connected in a large-scale area that is organized as a political unit. Some ideas are best shown by small-scale case studies of particular places in the country.

## Physical geography

A country's **physical geography** includes its rocks, relief, rivers, climate, soils and natural vegetation. These affect how people use the land. In Italy, for example, the Alps mountain range is a barrier to communications. In the past, this helped defend Italy from attack but also made it hard to trade with countries to the north. Today access is easier through tunnels built using modern engineering techniques, and the mountains are now popular places for holidays.

## People and the environment

Geography is also about a country's people – how they use the environment, and where they live. It also includes the work people do, such as farming, mining, industry, and office work. The geography of people is called **human geography**.

People have to understand the natural environment so that they can use it sensibly. Doing this in a way that can be **sustained** in the future is often difficult. In Italy, pollution caused by industry and vehicles is now a major problem in the cities, rivers and seas. This is causing problems that makes life unhealthy and unpleasant for people and wildlife.

## Using maps

Maps help show how the landscape is shaped both by natural processes and by people. Rivers, for example, carve valleys that are often used as routes for roads and railways. Rivers can also flood, which affects where settlements are built and how land is used.

Maps also give information that can be used to plan for the future. They show the best places for building and where building should be avoided. Different types of maps with data for the same area can be analysed to give useful information. Data in this form is called a **geographic information system** (GIS).

**A** Mount Etna volcano above the city of Catania in Sicily

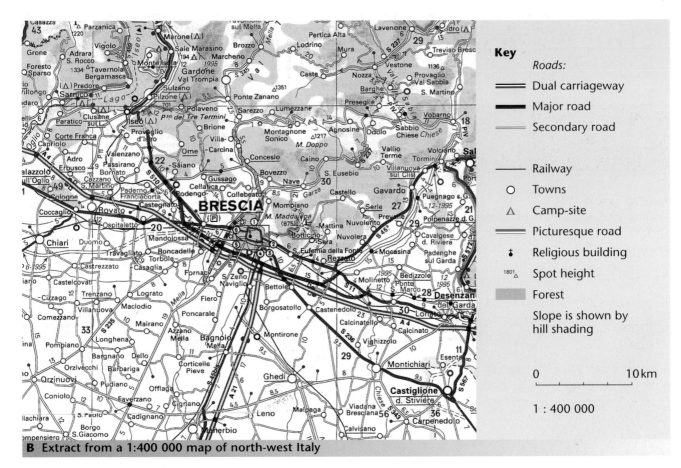

**B** Extract from a 1:400 000 map of north-west Italy

**Key**

*Roads:*

| | |
|---|---|
| ═══ | Dual carriageway |
| ▬▬▬ | Major road |
| ─── | Secondary road |
| ▬▬▬ | Railway |
| ○ | Towns |
| △ | Camp-site |
| ▬▬▬ | Picturesque road |
| ☨ | Religious building |
| $1801_\triangle$ | Spot height |
| ▓ | Forest |

Slope is shown by hill shading

0 ────────── 10 km

1 : 400 000

## FACT FILE

### The Lombardy region

The map above shows part of the Lombardy region in the north of Italy. The region takes its name from a German tribe which invaded the area and set up a kingdom in AD568. The Italian Alps are the highest part of Lombardy, with mountain peaks rising to just over 4000 metres. This area includes some of Italy's most beautiful lakes, including Lake Brescia.

Further south, there is low-lying land in the North Italian Plain. Italy's largest river, the Po, and its tributaries flow through the region.

The modern region of Lombardy comprises less than 8 per cent of Italy but has about 16 per cent of its total population. Some of Italy's most important industrial cities are in the region. Milan is the region's capital and is Italy's second largest city.

Brescia is the main city in Lombardy's Brescia province. There has been a settlement here since Celtic times, when it was call Brixia. It was under Roman control between about 200BC and AD452 when it was captured by Attila the Hun. Some of the city's streets still follow the line of the Roman streets. There are other Roman remains such as a theatre that was built in AD73.

Brescia became an important centre for trade and art during the Renaissance. There is an old cathedral from the eleventh century and a more recent one from the seventeenth century. There is also a fourteenth-century castle and a sixteenth-century town hall.

Today the city is a centre for industries such as chemicals and textiles.

# Italy from space

## Image of Rome

A **satellite image** shows a view of the Earth from space. Colours on satellite images are **false colours** because unlike photographs, images are made up from data collected by sensors. The sensors measure the amount of heat reflecting back to space from different types of surface. This process is called **remote sensing**.

The satellite image **A** shows Rome and its surrounding area. Rome is Italy's capital city. It is also Italy's largest city, with 2.7 million people. The river Tiber flows through Rome just after it has been joined by the river Anienne from the east. It flows in great bends called **meanders**. The city was first built on hills a few kilometres inland from the coast of the Tyrrhenian Sea. Now it spreads out in all directions, reaching out towards the Apennine mountains. The steep ridges and slopes of these hills make it hard to build on them.

## Volcanic past

There are many clues to show that volcanoes used to erupt in this area. Circular lakes and hills are old craters and volcanic cones. The widest craters are called **calderas**. The volcanoes in this area are now **extinct**, though their lava flows are still an important part of the landscape. The lava breaks down to form a fertile soil that gives a rich cover of vegetation. Rome itself is built on layers of ash that erupted from ancient volcanoes.

## Country land use

Large areas of the surrounding hills are covered by woods. There are patches of bare rock at the summits. Small fields can be seen on the lower land along the coast and in the wider valleys. The coastal area to the south of Rome used to be a marsh area named the Pontine Marshes. These were drained for farming about 50 years ago. The nearby Circeo National Park is an area where natural vegetation and wildlife are conserved.

### FACT FILE

**Satellite images**

The image on the opposite page was taken by a satellite in orbit about 15 000km above the Earth. The satellite collects data about how the land is being used. It does this by using sensors that detect the amount of heat that is being reflected from the ground. This is called thermal imagery. Getting data in this way is known as remote sensing.

Different types of electromagnetic radiation travel at different wavelengths. Radio waves have a long wavelength, while X-rays and gamma rays have shorter wavelengths. People can only see the visible light part of this radiation. Sensors are able to detect radiation at other wavelengths such as in the infra-red. The infra-red radiation travels in longer wavelengths than the visible light.

Measuring infra-red radiation is a useful way of collecting data about the amount of heat that is being reflected from the land.

A satellite image is made up from data about different types of radiation. The data can be shown separately, or combined to form a complete image. Different colours are used to show the different amounts of heat that are reflected. These are called false colours. This is why vegetation is usually shown in red on false-colour satellite images.

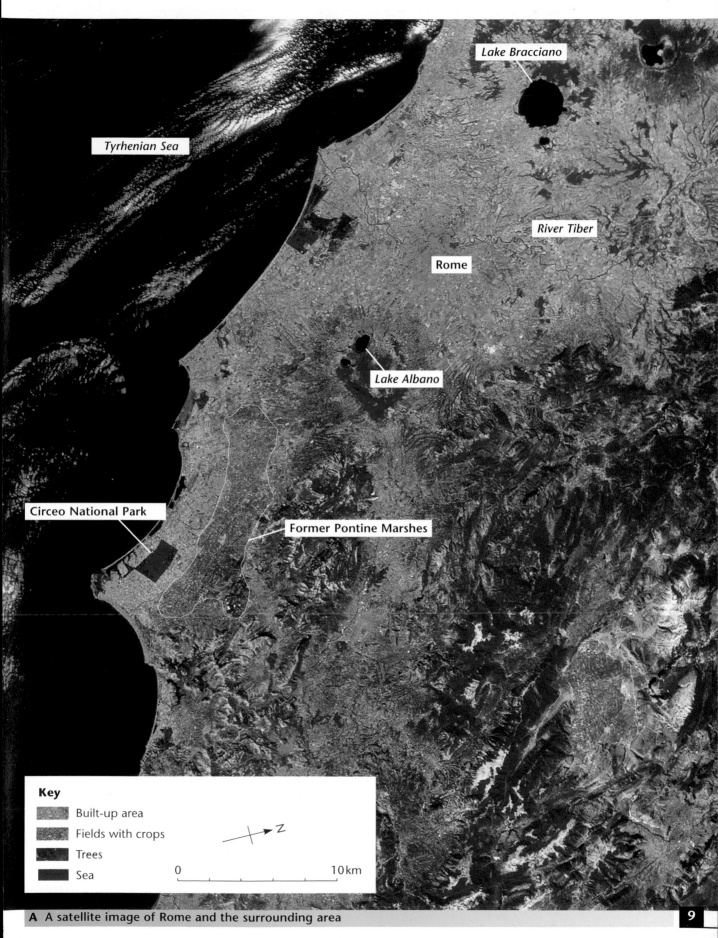

Lake Bracciano

*Tyrhenian Sea*

*River Tiber*

Rome

*Lake Albano*

Circeo National Park

Former Pontine Marshes

**Key**

Built-up area

Fields with crops

Trees

Sea

N

0                10km

**A**   A satellite image of Rome and the surrounding area

## Italy's physical background

▶ **What are Italy's physical features?**
▶ **How do Italy's physical features affect the country's land use and economy?**

### Italy's shape

Most of Italy is a **peninsula** that stretches from the Alps in the north to the island of Sicily in the south. The southern tip divides into what looks like a toe and a heel. The coastline along most of the peninsula has few wide bays and there are no long and wide river estuaries. The islands of Sicily and Sardinia are both part of Italy, as well as several much smaller islands such as Elba and Capri. Some of the islands, such as Stromboli and Vulcano, are active volcanoes.

### Mountains and hills

About 35 per cent of Italy is mountainous. The highest mountains are the Alps in the north. Monte Rossa is the highest peak at 4634 metres. There are deep valleys and lakes in the Alps, such as the Val d'Aosta and Lake Como. These were formed by **glaciers** during the last Ice Age. There is permanent snow and ice over the highest Alpine peaks.

**B** A road tunnel in the Italian Alps

The Apennines mountain range runs the whole length of the peninsula. Its peaks have a general **altitude** of 2000 metres. They are mainly made from limestone and sandstone. Some of the hills are the remains of extinct volcanoes. Vesuvius is the only active volcano on the mainland. Some circular lakes and rounded hills show where there is an extinct, eroded volcano.

### Lowland plains

The main lowland area is the Plain of Lombardy in the north. The rivers Po, Adige and other **tributaries** flow over the plain, forming wide, flat valleys. There are smaller areas of lowland further south such as around the Bay of Naples. Even the islands are mountainous, with only small areas of coastal lowland.

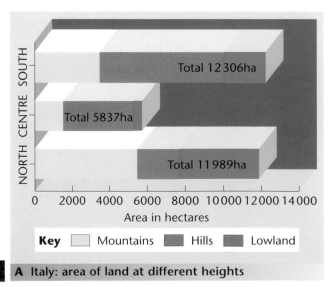

NORTH CENTRE SOUTH

Total 12 306 ha

Total 5837 ha

Total 11 989 ha

0   2000  4000  6000  8000  10 000 12 000 14 000
Area in hectares

**Key** ☐ Mountains  ▨ Hills  ■ Lowland

**A** Italy: area of land at different heights

**C** A river valley in Calabria

## Shape and access

Italy's **physical geography** affects how people use the land and earn a living. The long and narrow shape makes it expensive to transport goods between the north and the south. Access to the islands is even more difficult.

## Along the coasts

Italy has a coastline that is 4996km long. Beaches and small bays give opportunities for tourism. Small fishing boats use the bays as harbours. The larger gulfs such as the Gulf of Genoa and the Gulf of Taranto provide larger areas of sheltered water for shipping. The Mediterranean Sea has a very small **tidal range** which helps to make it suitable for both tourism and shipping.

## Effects of relief

Steep slopes and mountain climates cause problems for farming, industry, settlement and communications. The mountains are some of Italy's most empty and least wealthy areas. The mountain landscapes are, however, a resource for tourism. Winter sports such as skiing are a special attraction.

Settlement, farming, industry and communications are all easier on the lowland plains. This is because it is easier to build on flat land, and communications are also easier. Flooding, however, can be a problem in lowlying areas near to rivers.

---

### FACT FILE

**Italy's largest lakes**
**Lake Garda**
- Lake Garda is Italy's largest lake, at 370km$^2$.
- It is 54km long, 3–18km wide, with a maximum depth of 346m.

**Lake Maggiore**
- The name Maggiore means 'it is greater' (than some other nearby lakes).
- It is the second largest lake, at 212km$^2$.
- The northern end (41km$^2$) is in Switzerland.
- It is 54km long, with a maximum width of 11km and a maximum depth of 341m.

**Italy's largest islands**
**Sicily**
- Sicily is the largest island in the Mediterranean Sea, with an area of 25 460km$^2$.
- It is separated from the mainland by the Strait of Messina.
- There are mountains up to 2012m, with Mount Etna at 3340m, built up from the sea bed.

**Sardinia**
- Its area is 23 813km$^2$.
- The island measures 240km from north to south and is 120km wide at the widest point.
- The highest point is Punta la Marmora, which is 1834m.

# Italy's climate and weather

▶ **What are the features of Italy's climate?**
▶ **What causes Italy's climate?**
▶ **How does the climate affect people?**

## Climatic type

Italy lies between latitudes 37°N and 47°N on the south-western side of the landmass of Eurasia (Europe and Asia). This position means that it is seldom cold here, and often very hot. The climate over most of Italy is called a **Mediterranean climate**. It is similar to the climate in other places with similar locations such as parts of California, south-east Australia, South Africa and central Chile.

## Temperature and sunshine

The temperature in Italy rises to a maximum in July and August. It is a little hotter in the far south than in the north. Up to eleven hours of sunshine can be expected each day in Rome during July. In December, the average temperatures can fall to just above freezing point (0°C) in the north but are warmer in the south.

Temperature usually decreases with height. This makes the temperatures much lower in the high Alps and also in the Apennines.

## The rainfall pattern

The Mediterranean climate is known for its dry summer months. This changes in winter when belts of rain sweep across the country. In the north, there is rain throughout the summer months as well as in winter. The total amount of rain in the north is also greater than in the south. Thunderstorms are common during the summer months, especially in the north.

## Winds and pressure

In summer, a **high pressure area** usually spreads over Italy and most of the Mediterranean Sea. This brings slowly sinking air with clear skies and little wind. A hot dry wind named the **sirocco** sometimes blows north over Italy from the Sahara Desert.

In winter, low pressure areas called **depressions** often move across Italy from the west. These bring mild and wet westerly winds from the Atlantic Ocean. Rain falls along weather **fronts** between areas of warm and cooler air.

In some places, strong cold winds are funnelled through mountain valleys. These winds can blow at up to 160km per hour. This is strong enough to flatten crops and damage buildings.
- The **mistral** blows down the Rhône valley to affect Sardinia.
- The **bora** blows south over Italy along the eastern side towards Venice and the Adriatic Sea.

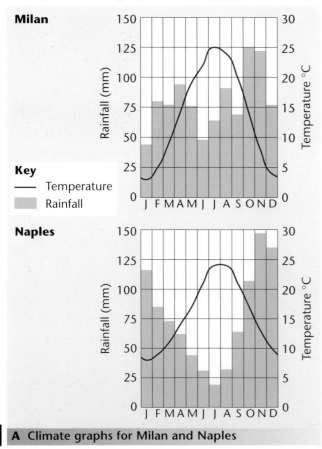

**A** Climate graphs for Milan and Naples

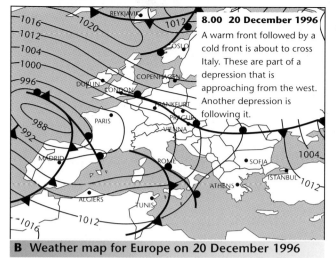

**8.00  20 December 1996**

A warm front followed by a cold front is about to cross Italy. These are part of a depression that is approaching from the west. Another depression is following it.

**B  Weather map for Europe on 20 December 1996**

## Climate and people

Italy's climate and weather affect people's lives in different ways.

- The extreme heat of mid-afternoon means that many shops and businesses close down for several hours.
- Winter snow in the north and summer sunshine over much of the peninsula helps Italy's tourist industry.
- The climate is suitable for crops such as grapes, citrus fruits and olives, but the summer heat and **drought** cause problems to farmers in the south.
- Industry is less affected by the climate, though air pollution from industry and vehicles is worse when air sinks in a high pressure system, trapping particles and gases.

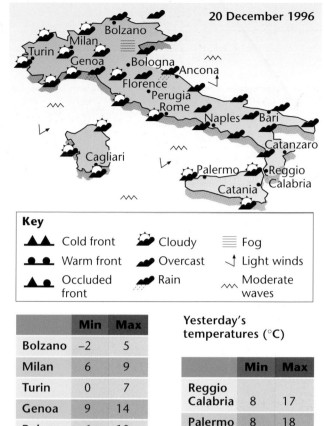

20 December 1996

**Key**

| | | |
|---|---|---|
| ▲▲ Cold front | ☁ Cloudy | ☰ Fog |
| ●●  Warm front | ☁ Overcast | ↗ Light winds |
| ▲● Occluded front | ☂ Rain | ⌒⌒⌒ Moderate waves |

**Yesterday's temperatures (°C)**

| | Min | Max |
|---|---|---|
| Bolzano | –2 | 5 |
| Milan | 6 | 9 |
| Turin | 0 | 7 |
| Genoa | 9 | 14 |
| Bologna | 6 | 10 |
| Florence | 9 | 13 |
| Ancona | 7 | 15 |
| Perugia | 4 | 9 |
| Rome | 3 | 14 |
| Bari | 3 | 16 |
| Naples | 6 | 17 |

| | Min | Max |
|---|---|---|
| Reggio Calabria | 8 | 17 |
| Palermo | 8 | 18 |
| Catania | 4 | 18 |
| Cagliari | 11 | 16 |

Maps **B** and **C** are from an Italian newspaper, *La Repubblica.*

**C  Weather map and data for Italy on 20 December 1996**

### FACT FILE

**Weather maps**

The weather maps for 20 December 1996 show that an occluded front is approaching Italy from the west. Both the warm front and the following cold front are about to cross from west to east.

The fronts are bringing long periods of low cloud and rain. There are light to moderate winds from the south-west, veering to the south as the fronts pass by. Waves in the Mediterranean are moderate. Temperatures are mostly between 3 and 10°C. There will be some fog in the north-east of the country for a time. Brighter periods with scattered clouds and showers will follow.

A second depression has already reached Spain and will probably cross Italy within a few days.

| | Milan | Rome | Palermo |
|---|---|---|---|
| **Jan** | 2 | 4 | 5 |
| **Feb** | 3 | 5 | 5 |
| **Mar** | 5 | 7 | 6 |
| **Apr** | 6 | 7 | 8 |
| **May** | 7 | 9 | 9 |
| **Jun** | 8 | 9 | 10 |
| **Jul** | 9 | 11 | 11 |
| **Aug** | 8 | 10 | 10 |
| **Sep** | 6 | 8 | 8 |
| **Oct** | 4 | 6 | 7 |
| **Nov** | 2 | 4 | 5 |
| **Dec** | 2 | 3 | 4 |

Average daily sunshine hours in selected Italian cities

▶ **What is Italy's natural vegetation?**

▶ **Why is there so little natural vegetation and wildlife?**

▶ **What it being done to conserve Italy's natural vegetation and wildlife?**

**A** Scrubland with deciduous trees, wild flowers and grasses

## The natural forests

There is not much left of Italy's **natural vegetation**. The natural vegetation is the plants that would grow in an area without being changed by people. Most of it has been cleared away by farmers over at least 8000 years. Only 23 per cent of Italy is now under woodland, and much of this is not natural.

**Deciduous trees** should cover most of Italy on both the lowlands and the hills, especially in the wetter areas of the north. Some deciduous trees have deep roots called **tap roots** that get water from underground. **Coniferous trees** such as pine trees should grow in the south in drier conditions on sandy soils. Their needle leaves help stop water from being lost through **transpiration**.

Trees that form the natural vegetation of Italy include these species:
• holm oak
• beech trees
• Aleppo pines
• Corsican pines.

## Scrubland

There is **scrubland** in places that are dry and rocky. Scrubland is mostly tall bushes and wild grasses such as lavender and thyme. This type of vegetation is called **maquis**. Areas of even shorter and more scattered vegetation are called **garrigue**. Types of cactus such as the prickly pear also grow in the Mediterranean

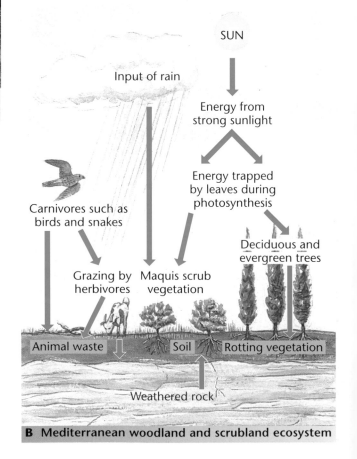

**B** Mediterranean woodland and scrubland ecosystem

**C** The Abruzzi National Park in the Apennines

climate. Their sharp spines are leaves that keep transpiration to a minimum. Moisture is kept in the fleshy stem.

### A Mediterranean ecosystem

The plants, animals and the soil that forms in the Mediterranean climate are all connected. This set of links is called an **ecosystem**. There are **inputs** of heat and rain from the atmosphere to make plants grow. Leaves and other bits of rotting vegetation fall to the ground. Insects and tiny organisms help break down the leaves and wood. These form **humus** and combine with minerals from **weathered** rocks to make the soil.

### Conserving habitats

Lizards, snakes, spiders, insects and rabbits all live in the Mediterranean environment. There are also some larger animals such as wild boar and deer. The plants provide food and a shaded shelter for these animals. This type of environment is called a **habitat**. The habitats of larger animals have mostly been chopped down.

Some habitats are now conserved in Italy's national parks and other conservation areas. The Stelvio National Park in the mountains of Lombardy is Italy's biggest national park. The habitats of animals such as roe deer, ibex, ermine and golden eagle are protected in this area.

## FACT FILE

### Italy's National Parks

Italy was one of the first countries in Europe to conserve land as National Parks. The Gran Paradiso National Park, in the Alps to the north-west, was created in 1922, followed by the Abruzzi National Park in 1923.

The largest Italian National Park is the Parco Nazionale dello Stelvio in Lombardy. This is in the Alps, and there is magnificent scenery here, as well as rare wildlife such as red deer, roe deer, ibex, chamois, foxes, ermine and golden eagles.

Just over 8 per cent of all Italy's landscape is conserved. The government hopes to increase this to 10 per cent.

### Rare wildlife

The chamois is a type of wild goat with short vertical hollow horns that hook back. The soft leather from the animal was used to make 'shammy leather'. This leather is able to absorb a very large amount of water, so it was used to dry and polish windows. Most shammy leather is now made from artificial materials.

The ibex is a type of wild goat that lives in the high mountains near the snow line. The males have enormous horns. They are rare, so are now protected.

There are now more wolves and lynx in Italy than there were ten years ago. This is because of better conservation laws and more tree planting.

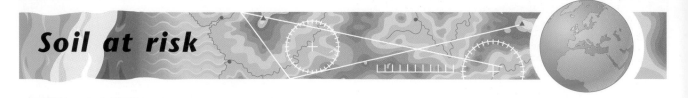
> ▶ **What is soil degradation?**
> ▶ **What causes soil erosion?**

## Soil degradation

Italy's soils have taken thousand of years to form from rotting vegetation and from **weathered** rocks such as lava and sandstones. But soil is easily and quickly ruined by different processes that cause soil **degradation**. These processes take nutrients out of a soil or break up its structure. This makes the soil useless both for natural vegetation and for farming.

Soil can also be blown or washed away by different processes of **soil erosion**. People also cause soil erosion, often with enormous effects over a short time.

## The effect of people

People affect the soil in several ways.
- The soil loses protection from rain when trees are cut down.
- With no rotting leaves, soil soon loses its fertility and becomes dry.
- Too many animals such as sheep and goats can cause **overgrazing** so that vegetation is completely removed.

In the past, farmers cut narrow steps called **terraces** on hillsides. Rain was held on the terraces. This stopped it from flowing down the slopes. But many of the small hill farms have been abandoned. Farmers have also cut away the terraces so that they can create bigger fields of crops, or vineyards. They can use tractors and other farm machinery in these fields. Without the terraces, the soil is easily eroded.

## Soil erosion

Soil erosion happens in two main ways.
- There is **sheet erosion** where soil is washed directly down slopes.
- **Gully erosion** is when a slope is gashed by small streams that flow over bare soil. Smaller gulleys join larger ones until the whole slope is stripped bare of its soil.

It is very hard to stop gully erosion once it has started. Gullies cut backwards into the slopes, so trying to stop further erosion by blocking them downstream does not solve the problem. More trees or other types of vegetation cannot be planted where the soil has already been washed away.

Between 10 and 150 tonnes of soil per hectare are eroded in Italy every year. Erosion is most severe where the slopes are barest, the climate is driest and where there are thunderstorms even in months that are otherwise mostly dry.

**A  The human causes of soil erosion**

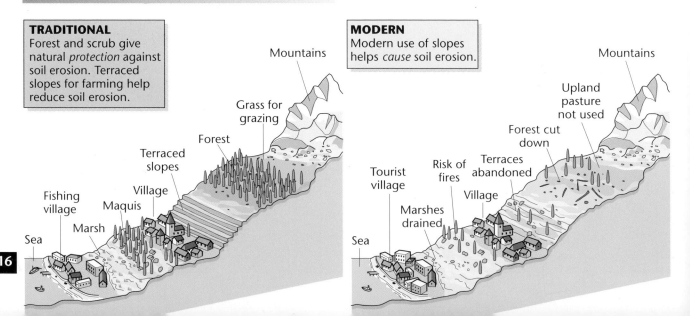

**TRADITIONAL**
Forest and scrub give natural *protection* against soil erosion. Terraced slopes for farming help reduce soil erosion.

Mountains
Grass for grazing
Forest
Terraced slopes
Village
Maquis
Fishing village
Marsh
Sea

**MODERN**
Modern use of slopes helps *cause* soil erosion.

Mountains
Upland pasture not used
Forest cut down
Terraces abandoned
Risk of fires
Tourist village
Village
Marshes drained
Sea

**B** Gully erosion on steep slopes in Abruzzi

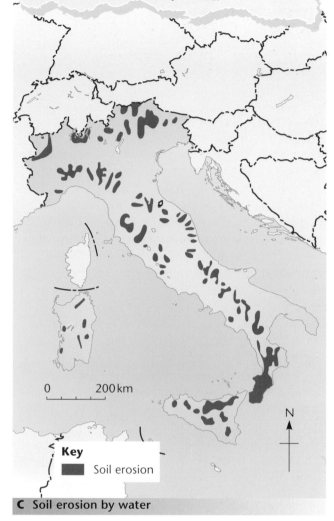

NEWSFLASH 10.2.96 Naples
After two days of heavy rain, a 40 metres high wall of mud slid down into the Bay of Naples. Vehicles were buried and pushed into the Bay with 5 people killed.

0          200km

**Key**

■ Soil erosion

**C** Soil erosion by water

The eroded soil is washed into rivers and transported to the lowlands. Some is dumped on valley flood plains where it forms deposits of fine mud called **silt**. The rest is carried out to sea or forms river **deltas**. Soil erosion is one of the causes of river flooding because river channels that should carry water become choked by soil and stones.

In some very dry areas the soil has dried out so much that few plants can live in it. This is an extreme form of soil degradation called **desertification**. Some parts of southern Italy are at risk from desertification.

## FACT FILE

**Saving soil**

It takes between 100 years and 2500 years to form about 2.5cm of topsoil by natural processes. This amount can be washed away in a very short time, sometimes as little as a few hours.

In Europe, about 1 billion tonnes of soil are lost by erosion every year. This is the continent that has the least amount of erosion in the world.

About 13 per cent of the Earth's land is at some risk. The hottest and driest countries, are the countries most at risk. In Europe these are countries such as Italy, Spain and Greece.

There are several ways to help stop soil erosion, or at least to reduce it.

- Trees can be planted to reduce the impact of heavy rain on bare soil. They also help to stop water flowing quickly down slopes.

- Narrow steps, called terraces, can be cut to break up the flow of water down a slope.

- Windbreaks help to stop the wind blowing away dry soil.

- The number of cattle, sheep and goats needs to be controlled so that grass and other vegetation is not completely removed.

▶ **What is the pattern of flow in Italian rivers during the year?**
▶ **Why do rivers flood, and what damage can they do?**

## Italian rivers

The longest river in Italy is the river Po at 650km. It rises in the Alps, flows across the North Italian Plain then enters the Adriatic Sea through a **delta**. The only other major rivers are also in the North Italian Plain.

Rivers such as the Arno and Tiber further south flow for much shorter distances. These mostly rise in the central spine of the Apennines then flow either to the Adriatic Sea or to the Tyrrhenian Sea. Many of the smaller streams and rivers in the south dry up completely during the summer **drought**. These are called *fiumare* in the south of Italy.

| Jan | Feb | Mar | Apr | May | Jun |
|-----|-----|-----|-----|-----|-----|
| 301 | 346 | 314 | 264 | 233 | 175 |

| Jul | Aug | Sep | Oct | Nov | Dec |
|-----|-----|-----|-----|-----|-----|
| 137 | 125 | 144 | 176 | 253 | 304 |

**A** River flow data for the river Tiber at Rome (cubic metres per second)

**B** A small river in Sicily, photographed in September

## Patterns of flow

The amount of water in most Italian rivers is very variable throughout the year. The annual pattern of flow is called the river's **regime**. The amount of water is usually measured as the **discharge** in cubic metres per second (cumecs). Changes in rainfall and temperature from month to month cause these differences. Occasional thunderstorms can make river flows hard to predict, even from week to week. Floods can happen because of thunderstorms, even in the driest months.

A **storm hydrograph** shows how a river's flow can change within hours of a rainstorm. Rivers with rapid changes are said to be 'flashy'. The floods they can cause are called **flash floods**.

### THE FLOODS OF 1994

*The rainfall figures*
On 5 November 1994, 150mm of rain fell on Turin. This was the highest recorded rainfall figure for one day since 1818. Rain continued to fall in the north-west regions of Piedmont and Liguria for almost two weeks. By 16 November, the rivers had overflowed and flooded the surrounding land.

*Flood damage*
Up to 100 people were killed during the floods. Factories, homes and farms were flooded. This included the Ferrero chocolate factory where damage and lost production cost 100 billion lira (about £4.2 million). One textile company estimated that it would take up to four months to get back to full production. Export orders were lost as goods were destroyed while waiting on lorries. Mud from the rivers was left everywhere. One reporter said it looked like a 'yellow-grey moonscape'.

**C** The effect of the November 1994 floods on Piedmont

## Flooding and land use change

Heavy rain is only one reason why there are floods. In the 25 years up to 1975, there was an average of 2.6 floods each year. The rate of flooding has now gone up to about three a year. Although the rainfall varies from year to year, the landscape itself has also been changed.

More building has been one of the causes of increased floods. Rainwater does not sink through **impermeable** concrete roads and other surfaces. Instead, there is rapid **surface runoff** as rainwater flows rapidly into drains and then into rivers. Too many new buildings have been built in the **catchment areas** that feed water to the rivers. Some of the building has been illegal, but little has been done to stop it.

**Global warming** may be another cause of flooding. Some scientists believe that this is making the climate warmer. It could also mean more rain and thunderstorms because of the rising warm air.

---

### FACT FILE

**The river Tiber**

The river Tiber was probably named after a king of Rome named Tiberinus, who lived about 3200 years ago and who drowned in the river. The Tiber's source is in the Apennines. It flows through Rome on its 450km route to the Tyrrhenian Sea.

The river is fullest in spring when there is rain and melting snow. Boats can sail on the river as far as Rome, but its depth and speed of flow are irregular.

The Tiber meanders in great loops, though its route is now controlled by stone walls through Rome to stop it from flooding. It has a delta at its mouth that has expanded by 3km since Roman times.

**Global warning**

Global warming may be the result of an increase in 'greenhouse gases' in the Earth's atmosphere. A greenhouse gas is one that lets heat from the sun come through the atmosphere as long-wave radiation. But heat that reflects back through the atmosphere as short-wave radiation is trapped by the greenhouse gases.

One of the main greenhouse gases is carbon dioxide ($CO_2$), though many other gases such as methane have the same effect. Many of these gases are put into the air by burning fossil fuels such as oil and coal, and by clearing forests by burning them.

# Sinking Venice

▶ Why is Venice at risk?
▶ What can be done to save the city?

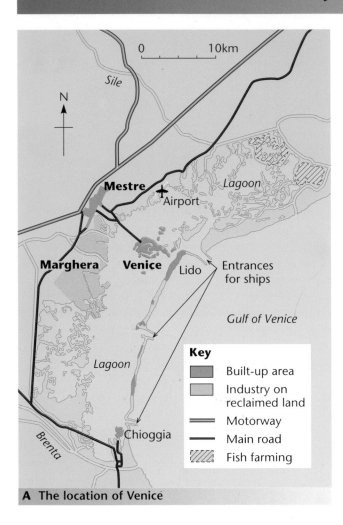

**A** The location of Venice

Key
- Built-up area
- Industry on reclaimed land
- Motorway
- Main road
- Fish farming

## An unusual city

Venice is one of the world's most unusual cities. Its **site** is in a **lagoon** at the northern end of the Adriatic Sea. At first, the buildings were built on wooden poles driven into the mud of the lagoon bed. Later, stone foundations were dropped onto the wooden base as buildings needed to be stronger. Venice grew during the Middle Ages to become an important port and commercial city.

Today, Venice has a population of 306 000. There are many fine buildings and squares such as the Doge's Palace and St Mark's Square. The Grand Canal winds through the city centre with many smaller canals branching off from it. It is one of the most visited cities in Italy, because of its many art treasures and historic buildings.

### Walking on planks

A problem is that the city is slowly sinking. The weight of its own stone buildings is partly to blame. Flooding by the sea has become so frequent that people are getting used to walking across St Mark's Square on raised wooden planks. Some art treasures have already been destroyed by flooding, and buildings are at risk of collapsing. Something has to be done if the city is to be saved.

### The rising sea

Flooding sometimes happens when a deep area of low pressure moves over the northern part of the Adriatic Sea. With less weight of air pressing down, the sea level is able to rise by about half a metre. This can combine with other conditions such as a high tide and strong winds from the north. This combination can cause flooding. Rising world sea levels due to **global warming** are adding to these problems.

**B** Historic buildings in Venice

**C** Flooding in Venice in 1992

## The sinking city

The city is also sinking because water is being pumped out of rocks beneath it. This is done to supply water to new industries at the nearby mainland port and industrial zones. Without the underground water, there is **subsidence** because the rocks cannot support the city's weight.

Another problem is that a deepwater channel has been dredged through the lagoon so that cargo ships can reach the port. The waves caused by these ships are eroding the building's foundations.

## Finding answers

Engineers cannot change the weather, the tides or the rising sea levels. There are some ways that the city can be saved but they would all need the agreement of the Italian government to use money from taxes. All of these methods would have an effect on other ways the area is used. The nearby port and industrial zones would be especially affected.

- Build flood barriers across the lagoon.
- Stop ships crossing the lagoon.
- Stop the taking of water from underground.
- Put in deep steel supports for the buildings.
- Stop **reclaiming** the lagoon for fish farms and other uses.

## FACT FILE

### Canals and causeway

Venice is sometimes called La Serenissima, meaning 'the most serene' city. There are ten main islands here and 45km of canals, divided into about 180 different parts, just like streets. The Grand Canal is the main waterway. The canals are about 3.5m wide on average. A black gondola is the traditional boat used on Venice's canals. They have been painted black since 1562.

In 1846, a causeway was built to link the main island to the mainland. A main road was not built until 1932. Now, however, cars are kept out of the main part of the city.

### The sights of Venice

There are at least 200 palaces and 10 churches in Venice. The Doge's Palace was first built in AD814. The Doge is the name for the ruler of Venice. The original palace was destroyed by fire, so a new one was built during the fourteenth century.

St Mark's Cathedral beside St Mark's Square was first built in AD828, then rebuilt during the second half of the twelfth century. The cathedral bell tower had to be rebuilt after it fell down in 1902.

There are two famous bridges across the canals. One is the Rialto Bridge across the Grand Canal, built in 1588. The other is the Bridge of Sighs, which leads from the Doge's Palace to the city's old prison.

▶ **What are the main geological structures of Italy?**
▶ **Why are there earthquakes and volcanoes in Italy?**

## Italy's fold mountains

Italy's mountains started to form about 30 million years ago as the African **plate** moved north towards the European plate. The plates are huge slabs of the Earth's **crust**. This movement buckled up the ocean bed and the thick layers of sedimentary rocks that were under it. The rocks were compressed and **folded** up to form Italy's mountains. Since then processes of erosion have started to wear down these mountains.

## Plate margins

The African plate is still moving towards the European plate at a rate of 2–3cm each year. The movement causes cracks called **fault lines** that break up the rocks. Movement along the fault lines means that Italy is a place where there are active volcanoes and earthquakes.

Vesuvius, Etna and Stromboli are some of the best known volcanoes in Italy. These are all still **active** volcanoes. There are many others that are either **dormant** or **extinct**. Volcanoes erupt when melted rock, called **magma**, rises through the overlying Earth's crust. The magma flows or is hurled out of the volcanoes as **lava**. Steam and gases also come out of the volcanoes.

Some of Italy's volcanoes such as Vesuvius can erupt violently and cause **natural disasters**. Others such as Etna pour out lava but are not as violent. Scientists still cannot accurately predict when a volcano will erupt. Magma movements between 200 and 300km below the surface are hard to monitor. Scientists can, however, measure earthquake shocks and changes in the height and slope of the ground. These give useful clues about a likely eruption or earthquake.

## Earthquake country

Earthquakes in Italy can be expected anywhere and at any time. The **focus** for an earthquake may be either directly under Italy, or many kilometres away in Greece or North Africa. The **shock waves** ripple out from the focus in all directions, shaking the ground as they pass.

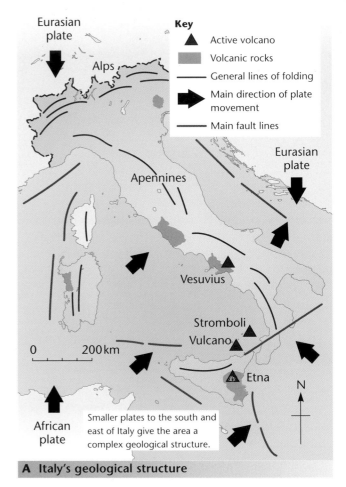

Key
- ▲ Active volcano
- Volcanic rocks
- General lines of folding
- Main direction of plate movement
- Main fault lines

Eurasian plate

Alps

Apennines

Eurasian plate

Vesuvius

Stromboli
Vulcano

0    200km

Etna

N

African plate

Smaller plates to the south and east of Italy give the area a complex geological structure.

**A  Italy's geological structure**

## Secondary damage

Some earthquake damage is caused by secondary effects. An earthquake can trigger a **landslide** or **avalanche** of mud, rock, snow or ice. This is especially a problem in the Alps where there are snowfields and loose **screes** of weathered rock. An avalanche can block rivers and cause floods. Dams holding back reservoirs can be damaged by an earthquake or by floodwater caused by a mudslide. This is mainly a problem in the high mountain areas.

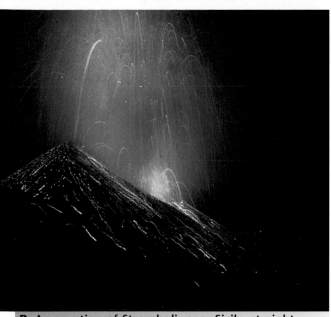

**B** An eruption of Stromboli, near Sicily, at night

A **tsunami** is a fast-moving wave caused by an earthquake under the sea bed. The Mediterranean Sea is not big enough for very large tsunamis to form, but they can cause local problems in coastal towns and villages. A tsunami can also be caused by a massive volcanic eruption. One of these happened in about 1470BC when the Greek volcanic island of Thira blew itself apart.

## Vulnerable villages

Villages built on hillsides in the Apennines are at great risk from earthquakes. Buildings can collapse when there is **slope failure** after broken rocks have been shaken. Whole villages have been wrecked and abandoned as a result of earthquakes.

Areas of low-lying ground where there is water in the rocks can be badly shaken by an earthquake. The ground becomes soft and unstable so that buildings collapse into it. This process is called **liquefaction**. Settlements in the north of Italy are most likely to be affected by this process.

**C** The village of Gibellina on Sicily after an earthquake

## FACT FILE

### Moving plates

The Mediterranean Sea is a shallow basin that has been left between the African and the Eurasian plates. The Alps and other mountains in Italy were formed when ocean sediments were folded up as the plates moved together. This explains why sedimentary rocks with seashell fossils can be found at the tops of the mountains.

Volcanoes erupt above places where the edge of a plate is pushed down into the Earth's hot mantle. The edge of the plate melts in an area called the subduction zone. The molten material then forces its way back to the surface through fissures or through a volcano's vent.

### Mount Etna erupts

Mount Etna on Sicily is one of the world's most active volcanoes. It has the world's longest written record of volcanic action, going back to 1500BC.

There are major eruptions with lava flows every few years, but most of the activity is much less. On one day in January 1996, for example, fountains of fire shot up from the volcano for six hours, sending molten material up to 300m above the crater's rim. Fallout of ash landed up to 12km away. The following month there were more fire fountains and falls of small lumps of molten material called lapilli. Some pieces fell up to 25km away on the town of Catania. In the past, lava flows have destroyed part of the city.

23

▶ **What natural hazards affect the Bay of Naples area?**

### Nightmare at Pompeii

The eruption of Vesuvius in AD79 is a reminder of the dangers of living near an active volcano. The Roman cities, Pompeii and Herculaneum (now Ercolana), were destroyed by eruptions that covered them with layers of volcanic dust and ash. People choked to death or were poisoned by the volcanic gases.

The modern city of Naples and other settlements are well in range of another violent eruption. The last major eruption of Vesuvius was in 1944. Since then, Naples has grown to about twice its previous size. Other settlements in the area have also grown. This puts an increasing number of people at risk. About 1 200 000 people live in Naples and a further 400 000 in the nearby Campi Flegrei plain. The volcano is sometimes closed off to visitors because of a release of gases, and other signs that it is still active.

### The earthquake hazard

Earthquakes in the Bay of Naples area are common, though most are too weak to cause much damage. Some are caused by movements along **fault lines**. Others occur as **magma** rises up into **magma chambers** beneath Vesuvius and other volcanic areas. One earthquake in 1857 killed about 12 000 people in the area. Most deaths and damage were in villages to the south-east, though the damage was spread over a wide area from Naples as far south as Calabria.

### Earthquake at Pozzuoli

The town of Pozzuoli sits on top of a magma chamber that is only 3.5 km below the Earth's surface. When magma rises in the chamber, the ground above it heaves up. It sinks back down again as the magma sinks. There are earthquakes whenever this happens.

**A  Satellite image of the Bay of Naples area**

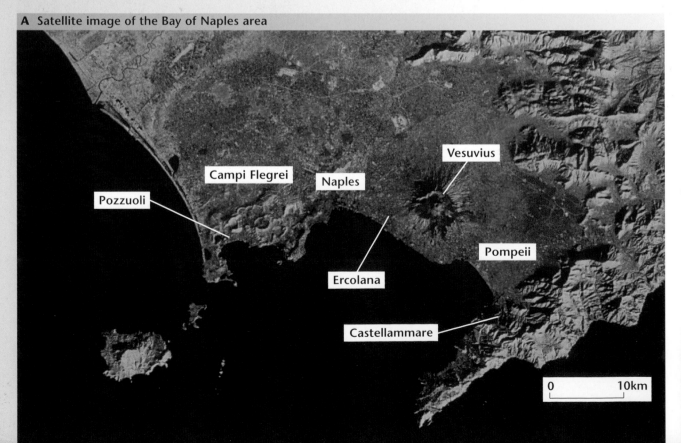

One of the worst earthquakes in recent years was in 1983. The ground moved up and down for several months before there was a major shock. By then, many of the town's 80 000 people had moved out and were living in tents. Even so, about 50 people were injured during the earthquake. The sea bed rose so much that the harbour became too shallow for some fishing boats.

Many people were so frightened that they left the town and have not moved back. Others have returned, either because they had nowhere else to go or because they are willing to take the risk that they will survive the next earthquake.

**C** Scaffolding holding together buildings in Naples damaged in the 1983 earthquake

**B** Vesuvius and the remains of Roman Pompeii

### Rising bubbles

Scientists are watching this area carefully to see if they can predict what will happen next. In 1538, a volcano erupted where the town of Tripergole used to be. This grew to become a 140 metre high volcanic peak in only three days. Bubbles of warm air sometimes rise from holes in the sea bed called **fumaroles**. This shows that heat and energy are being released from the rocks below. This may be a good sign as pressure is being released slowly.

A greater problem would be if pressure built up until there was a mud, steam and gas explosion. This could blast apart an area at least 2km wide. Scientists can only hope that this will not happen, but cannot be sure that it won't.

## FACT FILE

### Dangerous Vesuvius

The oldest known volcanic rocks forming Vesuvius are about 300 000 years old. Vesuvius itself only began to form after a previous volcano called the Somma volcano collapsed about 17 000 years ago.

Vesuvius is a 'strato' volcano, made up of layers of lava and ash. There were enormous eruptions in 5960BC and 3580BC. A Roman writer named Pliny the Younger described the eruption in AD79 in great detail.

The eruption threw dust and ash about 20km into the atmosphere. About $4km^3$ was thrown up over about 19 hours of eruptions. The city of Pompeii was covered by 3m of material. This type of violent dust and ash eruption is now called a Plinian eruption.

There was a major eruption in 1631, then another in 1944. The volcano now seems to be quiet, but it may erupt again.

# 3 ITALY'S POPULATION

## Births, deaths and population change

▶ What is Italy's total population and how is it changing?
▶ Why is the population changing?
▶ Are there differences in population changes between different regions?

### Zero growth

Italy's total population is just over 57 million. The population increased slowly during most of the twentieth century. But by 1996, the increase, as in many other **economically developed countries** (EDCs), had almost stopped. Italy's yearly population change is now about 0 per cent. This is called **zero population growth**. Now there are fears that the total population will start to go down.

### Births and deaths

Population change depends mainly on a country's **birth rate** and **death rate**. These figures count the number of births and deaths for every 1000 people in a year. The difference between the birth rate and the death rate gives the **natural increase** or decrease. The population total also changes because of **migration** between countries.

Italy now has a birth rate of 11 and a death rate of 11, so there is no natural change. This is surprising in a country where 83 per cent of the people are Roman Catholic. Roman Catholic teaching is against artificial methods of birth control but many Italians choose not to follow this teaching.

The change in a country's population is called its **demographic transition**. In the early stage, the population does not change much because there is a high birth rate and a high death rate. Then there is a rapid population increase as better health care makes death rates fall. Next, there is stability again as people have fewer children. Italy's population has gone through these different stages.

**Population total in Italy, 1951–95**

| Year | Population total (millions) | Increase of people for every 1000 people |
|------|------|------|
| 1951 | 47.2 | 7.4 |
| 1961 | 49.9 | 6.4 |
| 1971 | 53.7 | 6.7 |
| 1981 | 56.3 | 3.8 |
| 1991 | 57.1 | 0.3 |
| 1995 | 52.7 | 0.0 |

Notice when drawing a graph that the gap between all years is not the same.

**Birth and death rates in Italy**

| Years | Birth rate | Death rate |
|------|------|------|
| 1950–55 | 18 | 10 |
| 1960–65 | 19 | 10 |
| 1970–75 | 16 | 10 |
| 1980–85 | 11 | 10 |
| 1990–95 | 11 | 11 |

**A  Population statistics for Italy, 1950–95**

### Falling death rate

Italy's low death rate is mainly because of better medical care so that fewer babies die and people now live for longer. The average **life expectancy** is 73 for males and 80 for females.

**B** Mealtime in the home of a Sicilian family

## *Falling birth rate*

There are many reasons why the birth rate has fallen in Italy.

- In the 1970s unemployment began to rise after the world price for oil went up. People still in work felt too financially insecure to have more children, so the birth rate began to fall.
- More people moved from rural areas to urban areas. Houses in urban areas are dearer, and it costs more to raise children.
- More women now go out to work and have a career.
- Italian people have a special love of children. They find it easier to pay for just one or two children than to have a larger family.

- Many more children now live at home until they are aged about 30. They marry later and may not have children at all.
- People want goods and a lifestyle that they could not afford if they had too many children.
- There are now more abortions, in spite of the Roman Catholic teaching against abortion.
- There are few tax allowances for children.

One prediction is that, at the present rate of population change, in 100 years' time there will only be 19 million people in Italy.

## *A pattern of change*

Population change is different in the north of Italy from that in the south. There is a population decrease in most of the richer northern regions while there are still increases in the south. These differences are caused by the different lifestyles and the different ways that people respond to the teaching of the Roman Catholic church.

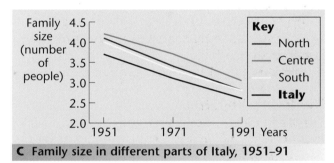

**C** Family size in different parts of Italy, 1951–91

## FACT FILE

### Italy's struggling population

An Italian professor named Antonio Golini has said that there is a real danger that Italy's population will keep on falling and will not be able to rise again.

| Million people | | | |
|---|---|---|---|
| **Germany** | 79.5 | **Belgium** | 9.8 |
| **Italy** | **57.2** | **Sweden** | 8.4 |
| **UK** | 57.2 | **Austria** | 7.6 |
| **France** | 56.1 | **Denmark** | 5.1 |
| **Spain** | 39.2 | **Finland** | 5.0 |
| **Netherlands** | 15.0 | **Ireland** | 3.5 |
| **Greece** | 10.5 | **Luxembourg** | 0.4 |
| **Portugal** | 10.3 | | |

Population totals of EU countries

| | Birth rate | Death rate |
|---|---|---|
| **Austria** | 12 | 12 |
| **Belgium** | 12 | 12 |
| **Denmark** | 11 | 11 |
| **Finland** | 12 | 10 |
| **France** | 13 | 10 |
| **Germany** | 11 | 12 |
| **Greece** | 12 | 10 |
| **Ireland** | 18 | 8 |
| **Italy** | **11** | **11** |
| **Luxembourg** | 12 | 11 |
| **Netherlands** | 13 | 9 |
| **Portugal** | 13 | 10 |
| **Spain** | 13 | 9 |
| **Sweden** | 13 | 12 |
| **UK** | 14 | 12 |

Birth and death rates in EU countries

# Population distribution

> ▶ In which regions of Italy do most people live?
> ▶ Why do more people live in some regions than in others?
> ▶ How has the population in cities been changing?

## Population density

The average **population density** in Italy is 194 people for every square kilometre. Since this figure is only an average, it means that some places have many more people and there are far fewer in others. The spread of where people live is called the **population distribution**. Natural conditions such as the climate, resources and relief play an important part in affecting where people live, but many other factors are also involved. These can be to do with events in history or culture, and different ways that technology can overcome natural conditions.

## Relief and climate

The least populated areas are the mountains and other areas with steep slopes. These areas are difficult to farm and have difficult access. The lowlands are easier to farm and are more accessible. This means that businesses are able to grow more easily and more people can live there. Bays such as the Bay of Naples have helped ports to grow where there is some flat land near the coast.

The dry climate of the south makes it hard to grow crops or rear animals. In the past, towns and cities depended on locally grown food. This helps explain the much lower population densities and lack of major cities in the south.

## Population and resources

Italy lacks most types of mineral resources including coal and iron ore. This meant that during the Industrial Revolution, industrial towns and cities did not grow as they did in the UK, France and Germany. Instead, Italy's industrial towns in the north, such as Milan, Turin and Genoa, have grown by using their good access, and **hydroelectric** power from the mountains.

## The urban population

In Italy, 67 per cent of the population live in towns and cities. These are called **urban areas**. The other 33 per cent live on farms and in villages in **rural areas**. The figure for the urban population is quite low for an **economically developed country**. The high percentage of people who work on farms in the south of Italy helps explain why it is so low.

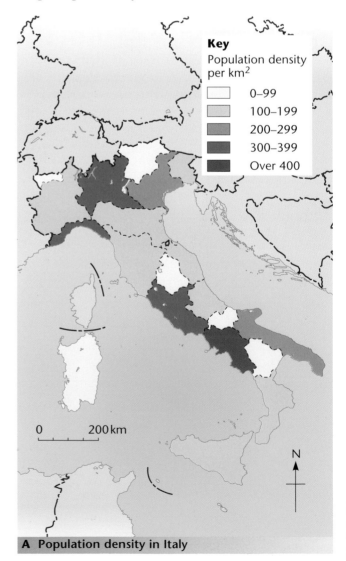

**Key**
Population density per km²

| | |
|---|---|
| | 0–99 |
| | 100–199 |
| | 200–299 |
| | 300–399 |
| | Over 400 |

0     200 km

N

**A** Population density in Italy

The population of the largest cities grew until the early 1990s. Now many people are moving out to nearby country areas. People are able to enjoy a better standard of living in smaller towns and cities.

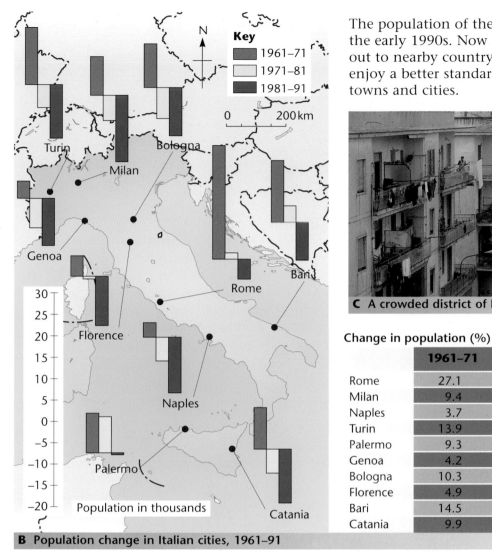

**B  Population change in Italian cities, 1961–91**

**C  A crowded district of Naples**

### Change in population (%)

| | 1961–71 | 1971–81 | 1981–91 |
|---|---|---|---|
| Rome | 27.1 | 1.7 | –4.9 |
| Milan | 9.4 | –6.0 | –16.1 |
| Naples | 3.7 | –1.3 | –12.9 |
| Turin | 13.9 | –5.5 | –12.8 |
| Palermo | 9.3 | 8.8 | –0.4 |
| Genoa | 4.2 | –6.9 | –11.1 |
| Bologna | 10.3 | –7.1 | –11.3 |
| Florence | 4.9 | –1.0 | –11.3 |
| Bari | 14.5 | 3.8 | –8.0 |
| Catania | 9.9 | –5.4 | –12.8 |

## FACT FILE

### Profile of Naples

Naples is Italy's third largest city in terms of population, with just over 1 million people. The people who live there are called Neapolitans. The name comes from a Greek word, *neapolis*, which means 'the new town'.

Naples is a port situated along the northern shore of the Bay of Naples. The central parts of the city are among the most densely populated urban areas in Italy, with narrow streets and crowded tenement blocks. The city has also spread out in all directions both along the coast and inland, including areas close to Vesuvius to the east and the active volcanic area of Campi Flegri to the west. One estimate is that within 15 minutes of a medium to large-scale volcanic eruption, about 1 million people living within a 7km radius of Vesuvius could be killed.

| % urban population | | | |
|---|---|---|---|
| Belgium | 97 | France | 73 |
| Netherlands | 89 | Italy | 67 |
| UK | 89 | Greece | 64 |
| Luxembourg | 88 | Finland | 62 |
| Denmark | 86 | Ireland | 57 |
| Germany | 86 | Austria | 55 |
| Sweden | 83 | Portugal | 34 |
| Spain | 76 | | |

People living in urban areas in EU countries

# Italian migration

▶ Why did so many people leave Italy?

▶ Why do people now move to Italy?

▶ What population movements are there inside Italy?

**A** An African worker in Italy

## Exporting people

Italy used to be known as a country that 'exported' people. A peak of **emigration** was reached in 1961 when just under 390 000 emigrants left. Between 1960 and 1962, 110 000 Italian emigrants went to Germany and 137 000 went to Switzerland. The reasons for such large-scale emigration were mostly to do with finding work.

- There was a lack of jobs and poor living conditions in some parts of Italy.
- There was a need for workers in other countries, such as Germany, to do low-paid jobs.
- Many people went to join family and friends in countries such as the USA and Australia.

In 1992, 57 000 people emigrated from Italy, of whom 15 500 went to Germany and 8900 went to Switzerland.

## Migrants return

Since the 1970s, more **immigrants** have come to Italy than emigrants have left. Many are Italians who earned enough money abroad to allow them to come home and start their own business. Immigrants have also come from countries in Africa and other **economically less developed countries**.

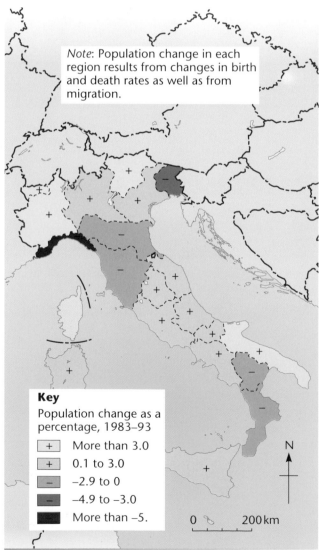

*Note*: Population change in each region results from changes in birth and death rates as well as from migration.

**Key**

Population change as a percentage, 1983–93

| | |
|---|---|
| + | More than 3.0 |
| + | 0.1 to 3.0 |
| − | −2.9 to 0 |
| − | −4.9 to −3.0 |
| ■ | More than −5. |

0        200 km

N

**B** Population change in Italy's regions

## Migration laws

Strict **quota** rules now limit the number of emigrants to countries such as the USA. But people from any EU country are allowed to move to any other EU country to work. This gives people more freedom to move and it allows employers to recruit workers from other EU countries.

## Internal migration

People also move between the different regions in Italy. About 4 million people migrated from the south of Italy between 1951 and 1971. Of these, 2.2 million went to other parts of Italy. They mainly went to Rome and to the industrial cities in the north.

In more recent years, fewer people have moved from the south. This is because new industries and other types of work have grown up in the south. There have also been problems in finding work and paying for housing in the north. Some people in the north even resent migrants from the south as they take many of the jobs and add to the general pressure on housing and services.

**The North**
- There aren't so many jobs in manufacturing in the North as there used to be.
- Housing costs are more there.
- There are better services there.
- It would be a move to an urban lifestyle.
- There are increasing problems of pollution there.

PULL

PUSH

**The South**
- To escape from poverty – though conditions here are improving.
- There is a lack of jobs here – but this is improving with jobs in tourism, for example.
- Earthquakes are a problem here.
- Many have already left farming, and numbers are still falling.

Should I... move to the North? Why? Why not?

**C** Moving between the regions

## FACT FILE

### Moving away from Italy

| Destination | Emigrants (thousands) |
|---|---|
| Germany | 15.5 |
| Switzerland | 8.9 |
| Other European countries | 6.5 |
| France | 4.5 |
| USA | 4.1 |
| Belgium | 3.7 |
| UK | 2.5 |
| Argentina | 1.5 |
| Canada | 0.8 |
| Brazil | 0.7 |
| Venezuela | 0.7 |
| Other | 7.0 |
| Total | 56.4 |

The destination of Italian emigrants in 1992

### Fleeing to Italy

In 1990 and 1991, refugees from Albania fled to Italy to escape from political and economic problems in their own country. In March 1991, 24 000 people arrived from Albania and tried to enter Italy. In 1992, there was another emergency when people fled from fighting in the former Yugoslavia. In 1997, there was more fighting in Albania, so more refugees tried to escape to Italy. Some had to be rescued from small and overcrowded boats.

Italy is also close to countries in Africa where most people have a lower standard of living than in the EU countries. Some migrants come to Italy in search of a better future.

▶ What might happen to Italy's population in the future?
▶ What problems can be caused by a fall in the population?

## The age–sex pyramid
The Italian government is worried about the country's population. At the moment, not enough children are being born to replace the present population. The number of children born to each woman is called the **fertility rate**. A fertility rate of 2.1 is needed to replace the country's population. By 1991, this had dropped to 1.27.

The **population structure** can be shown on an **age–sex pyramid**. This shows that the proportion of people under 19 years old is now down to 18 per cent. The proportion over 60 is now 20 per cent and rising.

## People, jobs and taxes
As the number of young people goes down, problems of unemployment may also go down. There may even be a shortage of workers, so wages could go up. This could make Italian businesses unable to compete with countries where wage rates are lower.

Fewer working people should also mean fewer people paying taxes, though higher wages should mean that people pay more in tax. A serious problem in Italy is that many people

manage to avoid paying tax. Instead, they work for the family and friends in the '**hidden economy**', where people do not tell the government what they earn.

**A** There is an increasing number of old people in Italy

## Elderly people
The percentage of elderly people in Italy is rising. Older people usually need pensions, more medical care and other types of services. The ratio of people who are earning and paying taxes to those who are not, is called the **dependency load**. With a high dependency load, the government may not have enough money from taxes to provide the services that everyone needs.

In some parts of Italy, the percentage of elderly people has increased by much more than the average. One region where this has happened is Liguria. Elderly people are attracted to live

| Males | Age | Females |
|---|---|---|
| 3.5% | Over 65 | 5.2% |
| 3.2% | 55–64 | 3.5% |
| 3.5% | 45–54 | 3.6% |
| 3.9% | 35–44 | 3.9% |
| 4.4% | 25–34 | 4.4% |
| 4.5% | 15–24 | 4.3% |
| 4.6% | Under 15 | 4.3% |

%5 4 3 2 1 Age 1 2 3 4 5%

**B** The population structure of Italy

there when they retire because it has a pleasant environment on the Italian Riviera. This puts a strain on local services such as hospitals and social services. The lack of young people also makes it hard for firms to find workers.

## More homes

Fewer people should mean less need for new homes. This, however, is not happening. There was an increase of 13.5 per cent in the number of homes built in Italy between 1981 and 1991.

This was an increase of 3 million, to give a total of 24.8 million homes. There are several reasons for the continued increase in demand for homes.
- The size of families is falling.
- People are living longer.
- More people now live on their own.
- With more money, many Italians want to buy a second home for holidays and for retirement.

Finding enough space for the extra homes is becoming a problem. Some planners believe that increased building has already led to an increase in river flooding.

### FACT FILE

**Living longer**

|  | % over 65 |
| --- | --- |
| **Liguria** | 20.6 |
| **Emilia-Romagna** | 18.5 |
| **Friuli-Venezia Giulia** | 18.4 |
| **Tuscany** | 18.4 |
| **Umbria** | 17.7 |
| **Marche** | 17.2 |
| **Piedmont** | 16.8 |
| **Molise** | 16.3 |
| **Abruzzi** | 15.5 |
| **Val d'Aosta** | 14.8 |
| **Veneto** | 14.3 |
| **Lombardy** | 14.1 |
| **Trentino-Alto Adige** | 14.0 |
| **Basilicata** | 13.7 |
| **Latium** | 13.3 |
| **Sicily** | 12.7 |
| **Calabria** | 12.6 |
| **Sardinia** | 11.9 |
| **Apulia** | 11.5 |
| **Campania** | 10.5 |

Old people in Italy's regions

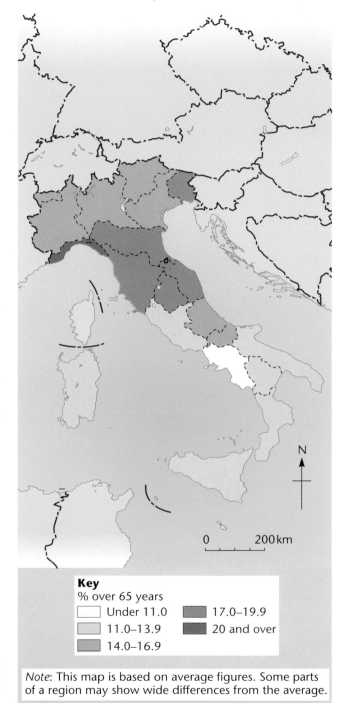

0      200 km

N

**Key**
% over 65 years
- ☐ Under 11.0
- ☐ 11.0–13.9
- ☐ 14.0–16.9
- ☐ 17.0–19.9
- ■ 20 and over

*Note*: This map is based on average figures. Some parts of a region may show wide differences from the average.

**C  The percentage of old people in regions of Italy**

# Population change in Calabria and Piedmont

▶ How has the population changed in Calabria and Piedmont?
▶ What effects might these changes have in each region?

## Comparing the regions

Calabria is the region that is furthest south on the mainland of Italy. It is one of the country's poorest regions, though people's standard of living has been rising. Piedmont takes its name from its position at the foot of the Alps. People's standard of living is much higher than in Calabria as there is more industry and there are more well-paid service jobs. The population in these two regions has been changing. These changes affect each region's economy, the environment, and every aspect of people's lives.

**Key**
- – - International boundary  —— Provincial boundary
- —— Regional boundary  ● Town

## FACT FILE

### The Calabria region

Calabria is the most southerly of Italy's regions on the mainland. It is also one of Italy's poorest regions. Just over 40 per cent of Calabria is mountainous, almost half is hilly, and only 9 per cent is lowland plains.

Only three major roads cross the 248km from north to south through the region. Two of these roads go along the coasts, with the third winding through the central hills and mountains. There are only twelve towns and cities in the region with over 20 000 people, and only three with over 100 000.

### The Piedmont region

Piedmont is a region with a varied landscape. Mountains cover 43 per cent of the area, 30 per cent is hilly, and the remaining 27 per cent is plains. It is one of Italy's most industrialized regions, where goods such as cars, chemicals, textiles, food and drinks are made or processed. Most of the industry is in the towns and cities. Turin is the region's capital.

About 44 per cent of the whole region's population live in Turin. This figure has been falling in recent years. This is because people have moved to live in less polluted, rural parts of the region. People have also been moving away from the region's other urban areas.

**B** Rocky hillsides and poor farmland in Calabria

**C** The town of Alba in Piedmont

## Population movement to and from Piedmont and Calabria, 1992

| | Moved to Piedmont from these regions | Moved from Piedmont to these regions | Moved to Calabria from these regions | Moved from Calabria to these regions |
|---|---|---|---|---|
| Abruzzi | 293 | 453 | 56 | 193 |
| Basilicata | 602 | 300 | 203 | 264 |
| Calabria | 3696 | 1830 | – | – |
| Emilia-Romagna | 893 | 1205 | 923 | 1851 |
| Friuli-Venezia Giulia | 257 | 354 | 103 | 197 |
| Latium | 1344 | 1785 | 1005 | 3226 |
| Liguria | 2905 | 2612 | 475 | 713 |
| Lombardy | 4519 | 4536 | 2409 | 6729 |
| Marche | 234 | 471 | 83 | 178 |
| Molise | 138 | 124 | 32 | 47 |
| Piedmont | – | – | 1830 | 3696 |
| Apulia | 3216 | 1943 | 496 | 563 |
| Sardinia | 1230 | 1240 | 96 | 71 |
| Sicily | 4387 | 3122 | 1164 | 1360 |
| Tuscany | 686 | 1188 | 480 | 1319 |
| Trentino-Alto Adige | 133 | 153 | 83 | 197 |
| Umbria | 137 | 174 | 56 | 241 |
| Val d'Aosta | 296 | 534 | 60 | 254 |
| Veneto | 706 | 1213 | 319 | 815 |

**Notes:** Figures are the total number of people who moved. The total numbers of movements are affected by the total population in each region.

### Age structure

| | Male % | Female % |
|---|---|---|
| **CALABRIA** | | |
| Under 15 | 22.4 | 20.7 |
| 15–24 | 17.8 | 16.9 |
| 25–39 | 23.1 | 21.7 |
| 40–54 | 16.2 | 15.9 |
| 55–64 | 9.8 | 10.5 |
| Over 65 | 10.7 | 14.3 |
| **PIEDMONT** | | |
| Under 15 | 14.3 | 12.7 |
| 15–24 | 15.1 | 13.6 |
| 25–39 | 21.9 | 20.0 |
| 40–54 | 21.9 | 20.7 |
| 55–64 | 13.0 | 13.3 |
| Over 65 | 13.7 | 19.8 |

### Total populations and density

| **CALABRIA** | | |
|---|---|---|
| Total | 2 079 688 | |
| | Population | Persons per km² |
| Cosenza | 785 000 | 118 |
| Catanzaro | 776 000 | 148 |
| Reggio Calabria | 592 000 | 186 |
| **PIEDMONT** | | |
| Total | 4 306 565 | |
| | Population | Persons per km² |
| Turin | 2 275 000 | 334 |
| Avercelli | 381 000 | 127 |
| Novara | 501 000 | 139 |
| Cueno | 546 000 | 79 |
| Asti | 209 000 | 140 |
| Alessandria | 445 000 | 124 |

### Basic statistics

**CALABRIA**

Area: 15 080km²

Population:
- 1982   2 078 400
- 1993   2 079 700

Density: 138 per km²

Provinces
- Potenza
- Matera
- Cosenza
- Catanzaro
- Reggio Calabria

Cities

*Reggio*
- 1982   174 100
- 1992   178 000

*Catanzaro*
- 1982   101 300
- 1992   96 890

**PIEDMONT**

Area: 25 399km²

Population:
- 1982   4 454 200
- 1993   4 306 600

Density: 170 per km²

Provinces
- Novaro
- Vercelli
- Turin
- Asti
- Alessandria
- Cuneo

Cities

*Turin*
- 1982   1 093 400
- 1993   945 600

*Novara*
- 1982   102 000
- 1993   102 766

**D** Population data for Calabria and Piedmont

# 4 THE ECONOMY

## Italy's economy

▶ **How is a country's wealth measured?**
▶ **How does Italy create wealth?**
▶ **How is Italy's economy changing?**

### Measuring the economy

In 1992, Italy had the world's eighteenth richest **economy**. One way to measure a country's economy and wealth is by its **gross national product** (GNP). GNP is the total value of everything that is produced. This includes all farm produce, factory goods and services. The profits from companies that work abroad is added in. The **gross domestic product** (GDP) only measures the wealth that is created within the country.

The wealth of countries with different population totals can be compared by working out the value that each person produces. In Italy, each person on average produces $19 620 of goods or services each year. This is called the GNP per head, or **per capita**. It is worked out by dividing the total GNP by the country's population. The figure is given in US dollars (US$) so that different currencies (types of money) can be directly compared.

**B** Canning tomatoes at a factory in Parma in the Emilia-Romagna region

### Types of production

Different types of production create different amounts of wealth. In Italy, for example, agriculture contributes about 3 per cent of the country's GNP, although 9 per cent of the people work in farming.

### Working in Italy

The jobs that people do can be put into one of four groups.

- *Primary:* jobs in fishing, mining, forestry and farming.
- *Secondary:* jobs in manufacturing industry.
- *Tertiary:* jobs in services such as in shops, hospitals and administration.
- *Quaternary:* jobs in high-technology industries such as working with computers.

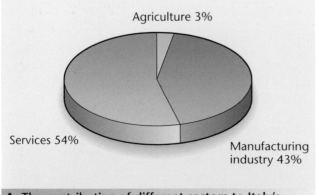

Agriculture 3%

Services 54%

Manufacturing industry 43%

**A** The contribution of different sectors to Italy's economy in 1992

The number of jobs in each group is always changing. In Italy and in most of the other **economically developed countries**, jobs in agriculture and manufacturing industry have decreased and jobs in the service industries have increased.

| | 1980 (%) | 1985 (%) | 1990 (%) |
|---|---|---|---|
| Agriculture, forestry and fishing | 14.2 | 11.1 | 8.7 |
| Manufacturing and construction | 37.5 | 33.2 | 32.4 |
| Services | 48.3 | 55.7 | 58.9 |

Note: Separate figures are not usually given for workers in the quaternary sector

**C Italy's employment structure**

One reason for this is that machinery has been replacing people on farms and in factories. Jobs have also been lost in manufacturing because of competition from other countries. Many of these are the **newly industrialized countries** (NICs) of the Asian-Pacific rim. Longer working hours, lower wages and poor working conditions in countries such as Indonesia and Malaysia mean that they can make and sell goods that are cheaper than goods made in Italy.

| (%) | Under 25 years | 25–54 years | Over 54 years |
|---|---|---|---|
| Male | 14 | 74 | 12 |
| Female | 21 | 73 | 6 |
| Total | 17 | 74 | 9 |

**D Employment statistics for Lombardy, 1990**

## The gender balance

Another trend in Italy has been for more women to be employed. In Lombardy, for example, the percentage share of women in employment has increased. This is because fewer people work in farming and manufacturing and more now work in service jobs. It is also because of changing attitudes of Italian women. Many now want to have their own career, as well as have a better standard of living.

## Unemployment

The unemployment rate in Italy is just over 11 per cent of the total workforce. Unemployment rose during the 1980s, but has now started to fall back again. There are great differences in unemployment between different regions. Another difference is that unemployment for women is almost twice the rate of male unemployment.

## FACT FILE

### Marconi's invention

Guglielmo Marconi was one of Italy's most important scientists and inventors in the present century. He was born in Bologna in 1874 of an Italian father and an Irish mother. At the age of 20 he began experimenting to see how far radio waves could be transmitted. At first, he could only do this for about 2.5km. By 1899, he was transmitting between England and France over a distance of 50km. In 1901, he discovered that radio waves could be transmitted for distances well beyond the horizon, and messages were sent from Canada to England. In 1909, he won the Nobel Prize for Physics. His experiments continued using different wavelengths and over different distances. He died in 1937 and was buried in Bologna.

| | GNP per head (US$) |
|---|---|
| **Luxembourg** | 35 850 |
| **Denmark** | 26 510 |
| **Sweden** | 24 830 |
| **Germany** | 23 560 |
| **Austria** | 23 120 |
| **France** | 22 360 |
| **Belgium** | 21 210 |
| **Netherlands** | 20 710 |
| **Italy** | **19 620** |
| **Finland** | 18 970 |
| **UK** | 17 970 |
| **Spain** | 13 650 |
| **Ireland** | 12 580 |
| **Portugal** | 7890 |
| **Greece** | 7390 |

Italy's GNP compared with that of other EU countries

# Farming and fishing

- ▶ How do natural conditions affect farming in Italy?
- ▶ What part do farming and fishing play in Italy's economy?
- ▶ How is Italian farming changing?

## The physical background

About 48 per cent of Italy is under **permanent cultivation** with crops or grazing for animals. The largest area of good farmland is in the North Italian Plain. Many other areas have slopes that are too steep and soils that are too thin for farming to be profitable.

The climate is a special problem in the south, where some areas have less than 600mm of rain each year. A lack of rain, together with high evaporation and temperatures of over 25°C in summer, causes problems for growing crops or grass.

Although 31 per cent of Italy's farmland is **irrigated**, poor farmers on Italy's many small farms in the south find it hard to pay for the equipment needed to irrigate their land.

## Patterns and changes

Different parts of Italy are best suited to different types of produce. Olives and citrus fruits such as oranges are mainly grown in the south. Grapes grow best in the centre and north. Rice is mainly grown on the flat irrigated lands of the Po valley. Wheat and other grain crops are grown in most areas. Durum (hard) wheat for pasta is grown in the south. Soft

**A   Farmland in Tuscany – with fields of grapes, olives and vegetables**

| Size | % |
|---|---|
| Less than 2 hectares | 52 |
| 2–20 hectares | 43 |
| More than 20 hectares | 5 |

**B  Farm size in Italy**

wheat for bread is grown in the north. The wetter north is best suited to dairy cattle.

Changes are slowly taking place in both farming and fishing in Italy.
- Some of the most unproductive farms have been abandoned or sold to make larger farms.
- Farmers use more machinery and more irrigation than in the past.
- There is overproduction of some produce such as tomatoes, partly because of guaranteed payments from the EU. But poor farmers need these payments to stay in farming.
- A special problem in Italy is caused by the Mafia who have acquired money from the EU farming funds by fraud.
- Fishing is having problems because of pollution in the Mediterranean and overfishing. More needs to be done to clean up the Mediterranean and to **conserve** fish stocks.

**Crop production, 1980 and 1994 (thousand tonnes)**

| | 1980 | 1994 |
|---|---|---|
| Sugar beet | 13700 | 12400 |
| Grapes | 13400 | 9400 |
| Wheat | 9300 | 7800 |
| Maize | 6400 | 7700 |
| Tomatoes | 4700 | 5300 |
| Olives | 3700 | 2300 |
| Apples | 1900 | 2100 |
| Potatoes | 3000 | 2000 |
| Peaches/nectarines | 1400 | 1700 |
| Oranges | 1700 | 1600 |

**Fishing catches, 1980 and 1993 (thousand tonnes)**

| | 1980 | 1993 |
|---|---|---|
| Trout | 25 | 35 |
| Pilchards | 48 | 35 |
| Anchovy | 79 | 21 |
| Striped Venus | 29 | 29 |
| Cuttlefish | 15 | 10 |
| Squid | 21 | 15 |
| Octopus | 21 | 17 |
| Shrimps/prawns | 11 | 14 |

**Animals on Italian farms, 1983 and 1994 (thousands)**

| | 1983 | 1994 |
|---|---|---|
| Cattle | 9100 | 7700 |
| Sheep | 9300 | 10400 |
| Goats | 1000 | 1300 |
| Pigs | 9100 | 8200 |

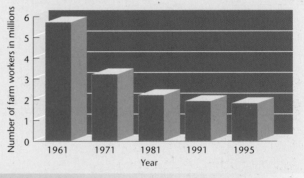

Changes in farm employment

**C  Farming and fishing statistics for Italy**

## FACT FILE

### Italy's wine regions
Wine is produced in every one of Italy's 20 regions.

The Chianti region in Tuscany is one of the most productive wine regions. About 100 million litres are produced in this region each year.

Valpolicella wines come from the Veneto region in north-east Italy. Asti Spumante comes from near Asti in Piedmont.

Further south, the mainly cheap white Frascati wines are produced in the Latium region around Rome. Even small islands such as Capri have their own vineyards.

### Food from Italy
Italian pasta is made from semolina that comes from hard durum wheat. This is mixed with water to make pasta dough. It can be made different colours by adding other ingredients such as spinach for green pasta, tomato for red pasta, and even the ink from squid, for black.

The dough is made into different shapes by squeezing it through different-shaped holes. Spaghetti, vermicelli, macaroni and ravioli are four common shapes of pasta.

Mozzarella is an unusual cheese made in Italy. Real mozzarella is made from buffalo's milk, but this is not always used in the cheese that is now sold as mozzarella.

## ▶ What are Italy's resources for industry and power?

### Rocks as resources

Italy has few types of rock that can be used as **resources** for industry and power. One exception is marble, which is quarried at Carrara. Marble is a **metamorphic** rock formed when layers of limestone are compressed and heated. It is used for statues and ornaments, and as a building stone. It is extremely hard and gives attractive patterns when polished.

Some sulphur is mined from the volcanic areas, but all of Italy's metal ores such as iron ore have to be imported. Importing basic metals amounts to 23 per cent of all Italy's import costs.

| | |
|---|---|
| Petroleum | 4634 |
| Lignite | 1075 |
| Pyrites | 377 |
| Fluorspar | 72 |
| Barytes | 52 |

**A** Italy's mineral resources (thousand tonnes)

**C** A petrochemical plant near Mantua in Lombardy

### Fossil fuels

**Fossil fuels** are rocks and gases such as coal, crude oil and natural gas. These were formed from the ancient remains of animals and plants. About 1 million tonnes a year of a type of coal called lignite is mined in Italy. About 4.6 million tonnes of crude oil is extracted, and some natural gas.

These amounts, however, are much less than Italy's needs to provide power for its industry, transport and homes. Even these small amounts will run out because they are **finite resources** that cannot be replaced. In fact Italy needs to import 83 per cent of its energy needs, mostly in the form of oil.

Some nuclear power stations were built in Italy, but only 4 per cent of the country's electrical energy is generated from this source. No more have been built in recent years because of safety fears after the 1986 Chernobyl nuclear power station explosion in the former USSR.

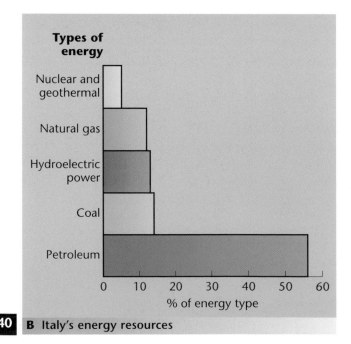

**Types of energy**

Nuclear and geothermal
Natural gas
Hydroelectric power
Coal
Petroleum

0　10　20　30　40　50　60
% of energy type

**B** Italy's energy resources

**D** An experimental power station using solar cells at Adrano, Sicily

## Renewable energy

There are **hydroelectric** power stations in the Alps and Apennines. Hydroelectric power is a **renewable** type of energy. It uses the force of rushing water to generate electricity. Many of the power stations were built in the early part of the twentieth century. The high level of **precipitation** and the steep slopes, especially in the Alps, give the right conditions for this type of energy.

## Geothermal energy

Italy was one of the first countries to develop **geothermal** energy, at Larderello in 1913. Steam from underground water heated by hot volcanic rocks drives turbines to generate electricity. This could become a more important type of energy in the future.

## Alternative energy sources

Italy does have some other options for generating electricity. **Wind turbines** could produce some energy, mainly during the winter months. **Solar power** could also add a small but useful amount. This area experiences 2000 hours of sunshine a year, and homes and villages in the south could generate electricity or heat water directly. Both of these are **infinite** sources of energy that do not cause air or water pollution. They are examples of **alternative energy** sources.

### FACT FILE

**Carrara marble**

Marble from the quarries at Carrara has been used since the time of the Roman emperors. The famous statue of the biblical character David by Michelangelo is carved from Carrara marble. The statue can be seen in Florence. It is 4.34m high and was carved between 1501 and 1504.

**Sicily's sulphur**

There are deposits of sulphur near some of Italy's volcanoes such as those in Sicily. Sulphur is used to make sulphuric acid and other chemicals. It is also used to make products such as fertilizers and matches.

**Useful volcanoes**

Hot mineral water from springs in volcanic areas is used for bathing, as part of the tourist industry and also for people's health.

Pumice is a volcanic rock which has holes in it where once there were bubbles of gas. After an eruption, rafts of pumice may float on the sea.

Volcanic rocks often break down to form fertile soils that are rich in minerals. These soils help produce good crops but they have encouraged people to farm on the slopes of active volcanoes. Eruptions can make this dangerous.

▶ **What goods are made in Italy?**

▶ **How do Italian manufacturers compete with companies in other countries?**

▶ **What is the workforce in Italy's manufacturing companies?**

## The growth of industry

Italy has a history of making goods such as cloth, glass and ceramics that goes back to the Middle Ages. Some of these **traditional craft** industries still remain, but they are mostly very specialized and on a small scale. Glass making in Venice is one example of these old industries.

**A** Printing onto textiles in a large factory

Now, **manufacturing industry** in Italy has become an important part of the economy again. It contributes 32 per cent to the country's wealth and employs 32 per cent of the workforce. International companies such as FIAT which makes cars, Pirelli (car tyres), Olivetti (computers) and Zanussi (electrical goods) are among the world leaders in these products.

## Adding value

Italy's manufacturing industry mostly makes goods from imported **raw materials**. The manufacture of cars, for example, needs imported iron ore and other raw materials to make the car's components. Making finished goods adds value to the raw materials. For example, value is added to cloth by making garments with designer labels, such as Gucci. Original clothes can sell for high prices.

Italian industry has a reputation for designing good-quality goods with style and imagination. These goods sell at high prices. Ferrari cars are a good example of this.

## Small-scale businesses

There are fewer than 100 workers in almost 9 out of every 10 Italian manufacturing companies. These companies often find it hard to compete with bigger companies in other EU countries which work on a larger scale and at lower costs. One way to compete is to pay low wages. At present, wages in Italy are among the

|  | World rank |
|---|---|
| Wine | 1 |
| Rubber | 6 |
| Petroleum products | 7 |
| Steel | 8 |
| Cars | 8 |
| Car tyres | 10 |

**B** Manufacturing production: Italy's world positions

| Year | % |
|---|---|
| 1980 | 37.6 |
| 1985 | 33.2 |
| 1990 | 32.4 |

**C** Employment in manufacturing industry in Italy, 1980–90

lowest in the EU countries. Some small businesses operate in the '**hidden economy**' and do not pay taxes, and sometimes employ children as low-cost workers. Low wages also give people a poor standard of living.

Small businesses in Italy usually have these features:
• fewer than 100 workers
• small-scale production
• a limited range of specialized products
• can change quickly to meet new demands
• work is done for bigger companies
• many are run as family businesses.

Behind this innocent façade, however, 20 shoemakers are at work in Dickensian conditions. There is no natural light, and eyes water with the acrid fumes of the glue. In the far corner of the room, I approach the small figure of Fabio, whose own shoes can only be a size larger than the child's boots he is making. The boy sits astride a vicious-looking machine which pumps holes into leather uppers. "I'm 14, I left school four months ago," he lies, under the suspicious eyes of the factory owner. "I like this job. It's fun."

From an article in *The European*, 12–18 December 1996

**D** Naples' 'hidden economy'

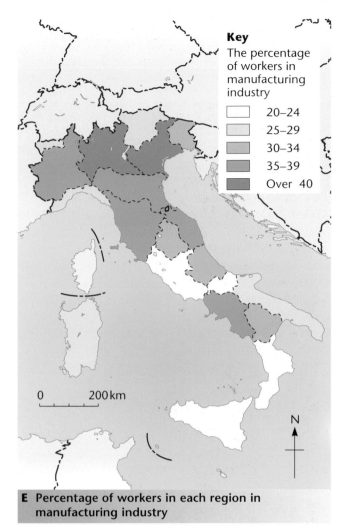

**E** Percentage of workers in each region in manufacturing industry

## FACT FILE

### Murano glass
There is a long history of making high-quality glass and glass ornaments in Italy. Most of this has come from the island of Murano in the Venice lagoon, where it has been made for about a thousand years.

Glass is made by heating together various inorganic elements, then blowing into the mass through a long hollow tube. The glass has to be kept hot while it is being shaped. The methods of doing this were a closely guarded secret during the Middle Ages. Murano glass-makers were not allowed to leave the area in case they took the secrets with them.

Murano glass is still made in the traditional way. It has a world-wide reputation for quality and artistry.

### The Armani story
There are 64 fashion houses in Italy listed on the Internet. These include names with an international reputation, such as Armani, Gucci and Benetton.

Giorgio Armani was born in 1934. The first clothes with the Armani label were produced in 1975. The clothes are usually first shown on the catwalks of the fashion shows in Milan and other centres of the fashion industry such as London and Paris.

Some of Armani's designer-label clothes are exclusive and expensive, while others are mass-produced and sold in high street shops and department stores. The Armani company also makes perfume and other fashion goods.

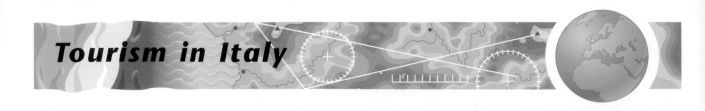

# Tourism in Italy

▶ **Why do people visit Italy for holidays?**
▶ **How does tourism affect the Italian economy and environment?**

## The tourist industry

About 50 million people visit Italy every year. Many come as tourists to enjoy the country's various tourist sites and attractions:

- coastal resorts such as Rimini on the Adriatic coast
- historic towns and cities such as Pisa with its leaning tower

**B  The small coastal resort of Minori on the Gulf of Salerno near Naples**

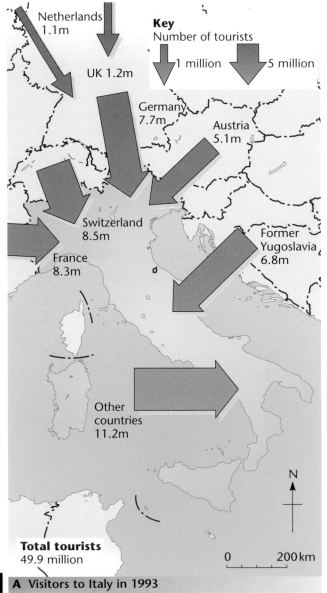

Netherlands 1.1m

**Key**
Number of tourists

1 million    5 million

UK 1.2m

Germany 7.7m

Austria 5.1m

Switzerland 8.5m

Former Yugoslavia 6.8m

France 8.3m

Other countries 11.2m

N

**Total tourists**
49.9 million

0          200 km

**44   A  Visitors to Italy in 1993**

- the capital city Rome where people can visit the Vatican City and ancient ruins such as the Colosseum
- the Roman city of Pompeii, which was destroyed by the eruption of Vesuvius
- rural landscapes in regions such as Tuscany
- mountain peaks and lakes such as Lake Como, which attract tourists for both summer and winter holidays.

## The effects of tourism

Tourism helps create jobs and brings money to Italy. Jobs are especially important in rural areas where there is often a high level of unemployment. However, most of these jobs are only **seasonal**. Seaside jobs, for example, are mainly from mid-July to the end of August.

Tourism brings changes to the environment. Land is needed for buildings and for roads. Better water supplies are needed and there are problems of pollution where new sewage treatment works have not been built. Traffic congestion in popular tourist cities such as Siena is a regular problem.

## TOURISM IN TUSCANY

The Tuscany region is one of the most popular tourist destinations. It attracts just over 1.1 million foreign visitors every year, with another 1 million visitors coming from other regions of Italy.

**C** Tourists outside the cathedral in Florence

**Landscape**
- The Apennine hills are mainly used as farmland with vines, olive groves, sunflowers and cypress woods.
- There are sandy beaches along the coast.
- Nearby is the island of Elba, where the Emperor Napoleon was imprisoned.

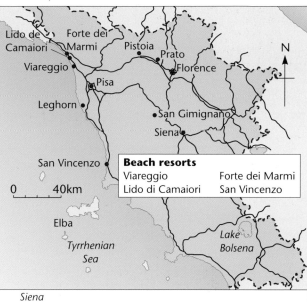

**Beach resorts**

| | |
|---|---|
| Viareggio | Forte dei Marmi |
| Lido di Camaiori | San Vincenzo |

**Historic towns**

*Florence*
- Buildings, streets and piazzas (squares) from the Renaissance period
- Cathedral of Santa Maria del Fiore
- The Uffizi art gallery with paintings by Leonardo da Vinci, Botticelli and Titian
- Michelangelo's statue of David

*Siena*
- A cathedral in black and white marble
- A 700-year-old university
- The *Palio* bareback horse race around the town

*Pisa*
- The Leaning Tower

*San Gimignano*
- One of the best-preserved medieval towns in Italy

## FACT FILE

### San Marino

San Marino is one of the world's smallest countries at only 60.5km² and with a population of 23 700. It is completely surrounded by Italy but it has its own flag, national anthem and government. Most of the country is upland, with hills and mountains.

More than half the country's wealth comes from tourism. It lies inland from the tourist resort of Rimini on the Adriatic. There are no separate passport arrangements, and people use Italian money, though San Marino does have its own stamps and coins.

The main city of San Marino is a well-preserved medieval city with a square, museums and churches. Another visitor attraction is its motor racing Grand Prix race track.

### The Leaning Tower of Pisa

The Leaning Tower of Pisa is one of Italy's most unusual tourist attractions. The tower is really a belfry, or *campanile*. Building work began in 1173, but had to stop after the first three levels were built. The tower had already started to lean because of ground subsidence. Building work was started again in 1275, and by 1301 six levels had been completed. The rest of the tower was finished in the fourteenth century.

There are 294 steps to the top of the 55m high tower. The top leans out about 5m from the vertical. The bells are still there, though they are not rung any more. Concrete has been pumped into the ground to stop it leaning any further, but other ways to stop it collapsing are still being considered.

# Transport and trade

▶ **Why does Italy need good transport?**
▶ **What does Italy trade with other countries?**

## Road and rail infrastructure

Most of Italy's main towns and cities are linked by a good **network** of modern roads and railways. Transport networks are part of a country's **infrastructure**. Good transport is needed so that manufactured goods, raw materials and people can be moved from place to place quickly and cheaply. This helps industries keep down their costs and their prices. Lower costs are especially important when a company is competing with other companies to sell goods all over the country and abroad.

Statistics for Italy's transport infrastructure show its main features.

- More than 300 000km of roads.
- 6200km of toll motorways (*autostrada*).
- 20 000km of railways, including high-speed railways which run at 250km per hour, and plans for high-speed rail links to France, Switzerland and Germany.
- 15 major seaports.

- Airports, including plans for a new 'Cargo City' at Rome Airport.
- In 1995, plans were announced for a new bridge or underwater tunnel to link Sicily to the mainland.

## Airports and sea ports

Rome's Fiumicino airport handles about 16 million passengers a year. Many of these are on international flights for reasons of both business and pleasure. Italy's long shape also makes internal (domestic) flights important. There are regular air services between Italian cities such as Milan in the north and Palermo on Sicily.

Major sea ports handle the country's **exports** and **imports**. Some of these, such as Genoa on the north-west coast, and Porto Foxi in south Sardinia, are for Italy's essential crude oil imports. La Spezia, also on the north-west coast, is a **container port** handling a wide range of goods. Ferry ports link the mainland to islands such as Sardinia and Sicily.

**A  The central railway station in Milan**

## Imports and exports

Raw materials and many types of manufactured goods are imported to Italy. Raw materials are needed for Italy's industries. Goods such as clothes, food and cars are imported because Italians demand a wide choice of goods to buy. Buying goods from other countries means that money leaves Italy.

Italy exports goods to other countries to bring money into the country. Money is also brought into Italy by tourists. The difference between the value of the imports and the value of the exports gives a country's **balance of payments**. It is best to have more money coming in than going out.

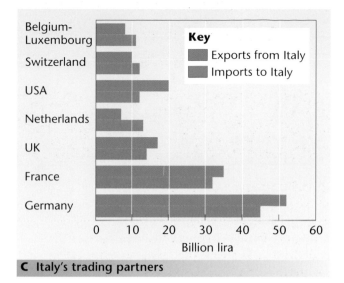

**C  Italy's trading partners**

| | Imports | Exports |
|---|---|---|
| Machinery | 41 | 74 |
| Road vehicles | 36 | 18 |
| Chemicals | 28 | 20 |
| Food and live animals | 26 | 15 |
| Transport equipment | 25 | 24 |
| Mineral fuels (oil) | 22 | – |
| **Total** | **232** | **265** |

**B  Italy's imports and exports (billion lira)**

## Trading partners

Most of Italy's trade is now with the other EU countries such as Germany and France. EU rules do not allow taxes to be put on goods

imported from other EU countries. This means that the companies in Italy must make and sell their goods at prices that can compete with goods made in other EU countries.

Some imports, such as raw materials and fuels, come from countries outside the EU. Import taxes on raw materials are usually very low or there are none at all, but taxes on imported manufactured goods are usually much higher. There are import taxes of up to 14 per cent for imported textiles and electronic goods. This is done to help protect jobs in manufacturing industry in Italy. Import taxes make it hard for other countries such as those in Africa and Asia to build up their own manufacturing industry and sell goods abroad.

## FACT FILE

**Building tunnels**
The 13.7km Mont Cenis railway tunnel through the Alps between Italy and France was built in 1871.

In 1922, a 19.8km railway tunnel was built to link Italy and Switzerland under the Simplon Pass. An 11.6km road tunnel was built through Mont Blanc in 1965, and in 1980 the 13km Fréjus tunnel was built.

The longest road tunnel is the 16.3km tunnel under the St Gotthard Pass to Switzerland. This was started in 1969 and was opened in 1980. Nineteen workers were killed during the building of the tunnel.

**EU trade**

| | Imports | Exports |
|---|---|---|
| Austria | 54 | 44 |
| Belgium/Luxembourg | 125 | 123 |
| Denmark | 34 | 40 |
| Finland | 21 | 24 |
| France | 239 | 232 |
| Germany | 408 | 430 |
| Greece | 22 | 9 |
| Ireland | 22 | 28 |
| **Italy** | **189** | **178** |
| Netherlands | 134 | 140 |
| Portugal | 31 | 19 |
| Spain | 100 | 64 |
| Sweden | 50 | 56 |
| UK | 222 | 190 |

Imports and exports of the EU countries (thousand million US$)

# The FIAT company

> ▶ **What are the characteristics of FIAT, Italy's leading vehicle-making company?**
>
> ▶ **How important is FIAT to jobs and the economy in Italy?**

## FIAT products

The letters FIAT spell the Fabbrica Italiani Automobile Torino. FIAT began making cars in 1899 in Turin. Now it also makes all types of other vehicles such as lorries, buses, tractors, trains and aircraft. FIAT has bought up other car companies such as Lancia, Ferrari, Alfa Romeo and Masserati, though they still use these old company names.

- FIAT gives Italy 4.3% of the country's GDP.

- It employs 4.9% of all Italy's industrial workers.

- Products exported by FIAT companies were worth 12 500 billion lira in 1995.

**A FIAT and the Italian economy**

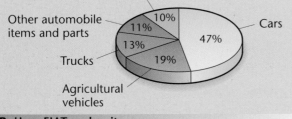

Aircraft, trains, publishing, insurance and other services

Other automobile items and parts — 11%

10%

Cars — 47%

13%

Trucks — 19%

Agricultural vehicles

**B How FIAT makes its money**

FIAT also makes parts for its own cars and for those of other companies. It makes dashboards, air-conditioning systems, cylinder heads and many other items. The company works on **joint ventures** with companies in other countries, such as on the new Eurofighter aircraft. This helps make savings on the high costs of developing a new product, and helps get bigger sales. Some FIAT cars are made under **licence** in other countries.

Many of FIAT's products have nothing to do with vehicles, for example making heart pacemakers, chemicals, and artificial cloth.

FIAT also has interests in property, publishing, insurance and other financial services.

## FIAT locations

FIAT's headquarters and main car factory are still in Turin. There are also factories in Milan and other cities. FIAT is located in the north for several reasons:
- a skilled local workforce
- a good industrial infrastructure
- sales to Italy's wealthiest regions
- links with nearby component suppliers
- easy access to other European countries.

There are also car assembly plants in the south of Italy, including a new factory at Melfi where 450 000 cars will be made each year. There is another new factory at Pratola Sera in the Molise region where 3000 engines will be made each day. There are good reasons for locating new factories in the south:
- cheap land on 'greenfield' sites (land with no buildings)
- wage rates are low in the south
- government and EU grants available to locate in regions with high unemployment.

FIAT owns factories in 59 other countries, in North and South America, Africa, Asia, Australia and Europe. The Palio project aims to make a 'world car'. This could be built in as many as 13 different countries.

**C A FIAT jet fighter**

## Cars and the environment

Levels of different types of air pollution have been rising in Italy. Carbon dioxide emissions went up by about one-third between 1985 and 1990, mainly from vehicles. FIAT is designing cars that will run on electric batteries, and others on natural gas, and buses and trucks that will run on natural gas. These designs may help keep the company ahead in the future.

FIAT also has a scheme to recycle parts of old cars. Foam from seats can be used to make carpets, while glass and metal parts can be melted down to make new metal and glass. Plastic parts can be broken down to make other chemicals.

### FACT FILES

**FIAT facts**

FIAT . . .

- has 2700 robots at work in its factories
- has 220 factories in 20 countries
- makes solid boosters for the Ariane rockets, at Colleferro near Rome
- has a 21 per cent share in the Eurofighter and a 15 per cent share in the Tornado combat aircraft
- has made tilting high-speed trains, with 44 in operation in Germany, Switzerland, Spain and other countries, with more than 100 trains on order
- has made 195 000 heart pacemakers and 140 000 heart valves since 1977
- owns the newspaper *La Stampa*, which sells about 406 000 copies every day.

|  | Millions |
|---|---|
| Japan | 8.7 |
| USA | 5.7 |
| Germany | 3.9 |
| France | 2.9 |
| South Korea | 1.5 |
| Spain | 1.5 |
| UK | 1.3 |
| Italy | 1.1 |
| Canada | 1.1 |
| Russia | 1.0 |

World production of cars, 1991

**Total employment 1993–95**

| 1993 | 260 900 |
| 1994 | 248 200 |
| 1995 | 236 800 |

**Employment by country**

| Northern Italy | 105 800 |
| Southern Italy | 44 400 |
| In other European countries | 50 700 |
| Rest of the world | 35 900 |
| **Total** | **236 800** |

An additional 425 000 people work in dealerships and in other companies related to FIAT.

**D  Employment by FIAT**

| Cars | 2 331 000 |
| Trucks | 174 000 |
| Agricultural tractors | 116 000 |

**E  FIAT and joint-venture sales in 1995**

| Cars | 11% |
| Light commercial vehicles | 17% |
| Trucks | 16% |
| Buses and coaches | 11% |
| Agricultural tractors | 21% |
| Combine harvesters | 26% |
| Construction equipment | 11% |

**F  FIAT's sales in other West European countries**

| **Trucks** | |
| Argentina | 13% |
| Turkey | 22% |
| India | 23% |
| Australia | 20% |
| Egypt | 15% |
| Libya | 88% |
| Tunisia | 40% |
| Venezuela | 22% |
| **Cars** | |
| Brazil | 28% |
| Poland | 51% |
| Argentina | 28% |
| Turkey | 44% |
| South Africa | 7% |

**G  FIAT's sales in other countries**

# 5 ▶ REGIONAL CONTRASTS

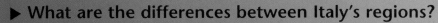

## *Causes and problems*

▶ **What are the differences between Italy's regions?**
▶ **What problems do regional differences cause?**
▶ **Why are there differences between regions?**

## Different regions

Some Italian people feel that Italy should be divided into two countries. One small political party called the Lega Lombarda want to make the north a separate country. They think that the north's economy and standard of living would be much higher if it were not joined to the south.

There are differences in employment and in people's standard of living between Italy's regions. The types of work, the amount of unemployment and the wages that are paid are different. In general, there is more wealth in the north than in the south. The differences can be seen in the wealth of Milan's shopping arcades compared with the poverty in the back streets of Naples or the other cities in the south. The amount of poverty in southern Italy is not as great as it was 20 years ago, but the differences between north and south still remain.

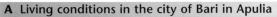

**A Living conditions in the city of Bari in Apulia**

## The regional problem

Great contrasts between regions can cause problems that governments usually try to avoid. By 1960, there were four main problems in Italy.

*   The degree of poverty and the number of people affected in the south was too great for a modern industrial country.
*   Migration from the south was causing problems of housing and unemployment in the north.
*   The youngest and most active workers were moving away from the south.
*   Governments need people's votes in all parts of the country to stay in power and to keep the country together.

## Causes of contrasts

In Italy, there is a long history of differences between regions in the north and regions in the south. The regions to the south of Rome are called the **Mezzogiorno**. Reasons for differences between regions are often complex. Some are caused by events in history, others by the physical geography and location. There are also differences caused by people's values and beliefs.

### Climate and relief

*   The south of Italy has a climate and landscape that is difficult for farming, so country people have stayed poor.
*   The climate and relief is more favourable to farming in the north.

### Owning land

*   In the south, much of the land was owned by rich landowners who rented land to peasant farmers or who used hired workers.

**B** High-quality shops in a shopping mall in Milan

- In the north, people either owned their own land or were more used to working in commerce and industry.

## Access
- The south is furthest from the rest of mainland Europe.
- The north has easier access to other countries for trade.

## Resources and energy
- The south lacks large amounts of mineral and energy resources.
- The north lacks mineral resources, but there is hydroelectric power from the mountains.

## Industrial growth
- There have been no major centres of industry in the south.
- Cities in the north became industrial centres then attracted more growth to them because of their success.

## Religious beliefs
- The influence of Roman Catholic teaching on birth control is greatest in the south.
- Fewer people in the north practise all the teachings of the Roman Catholic Church on birth control.

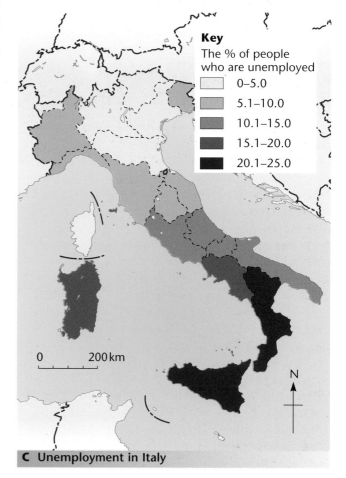

**Key**
The % of people who are unemployed

- 0–5.0
- 5.1–10.0
- 10.1–15.0
- 15.1–20.0
- 20.1–25.0

0  200 km

N

**C** Unemployment in Italy

---

### FACT FILE

**A divided country**

In the regional government elections of 1990, about 20 per cent of the voters in the north voted for the Lega Lombarda political party. Voters were voting for a political party that wants to make the north of Italy into a separate country.

| % unemployed in 1994 | | | |
|---|---|---|---|
| Abruzzi | 9.4 | Marche | 6.6 |
| Apulia | 16.8 | Molise | 16.5 |
| Basilicata | 17.9 | Piedmont | 8.4 |
| Calabria | 23.3 | Sardinia | 21.0 |
| Campania | 25.3 | Trentino-Alto Adige | 4.2 |
| Emilia-Romagna | 6.1 | Tuscany | 8.5 |
| Friuli-Venezia Giulia | 7.4 | Umbria | 9.7 |
| Latium | 12.7 | Val d'Aosta | 5.6 |
| Liguria | 11.7 | Veneto | 5.6 |
| Lombardy | 6.2 | | |

Unemployment in Italy's regions

# Contrasts in farming

## ▶ In what ways is farming different in different regions of Italy?

### Farms in the north

Some of the most extreme contrasts between regions can be seen in the way people farm the land. Farming in the north is mostly on small farms but they are modern and **capital intensive**, with money spent on machinery, fertilizers and technology. Most farms in the north are run as profitable **commercial** businesses. Production is **intensive** with high crop **yields** from every hectare.

### Farms in the south

In the south, farming is more **labour intensive**. Many farmers do not earn enough to buy much machinery or to improve their land. The farms are mostly small with fields that are small and scattered. There are some larger farms where sheep graze over areas of poor ground. This is called **extensive** farming.

Some farmers work in factories at other jobs, then work on their farm in the evening and at weekends. Money paid by the EU for produce and as **subsidies** helps these farms to survive. One reason for these payments has been to stop **rural depopulation** and to help poor people make a living.

| Average size: | 9 hectares |
|---|---|
| Soils: | fertile alluvial soils in the North Italian Plain |
| Main produce: | maize, wheat, rice, barley, oats, potatoes, vegetables, milk and pigs |
| Labour: | 1 worker on each farm |
| Methods: | use of machinery and fertilizers, both natural and chemical |
| Markets: | sale of produce to food-processing factories and shops |

**A  Farming in Lombardy**

| Average size: | 4.5 hectares |
|---|---|
| Soils: | thin, dry and often infertile soils in an area that is mainly mountain and hills |
| Main produce: | cereals, vegetables, fruits, olives, vines, sheep |
| Labour: | run by the family, often as a part-time business |
| Methods: | traditional methods with some irrigation |
| Markets: | food-processing factories for olives and grapes, exports of citrus fruits and local markets for vegetables |

**C  Farming in Calabria**

## FACT FILE

### The Calabrian map

The villages of Bivongi, Razzano and Stilo are located in an upland area of Calabria. Spot heights show that the hilltops rise to about 300 metres. Contours close together show that most of the land is steep. Steep mountain streams rush down narrow valleys towards the coast. The village of Stilo is reached by a winding main road. The other villages are in valley bottoms.

Cypress, oak and other trees grow in scattered patches. There are citrus groves in the valley bottoms. Sheep farming is common, though every type of farming is difficult.

### The Lombardy map

Limena is a village at the eastern end of the North Italian Plain in Lombardy. The wide, meandering river Brenta flows through the landscape on its way to the Adriatic Sea. The land in this area is mostly at about 20m. The lack of contours shows that the land is either flat or has only very gentle slopes.

There are few trees in this area, as most of the land is used for farming. Large rectangular fields take up most of the land. Much of it is used as vineyards for growing grapes.

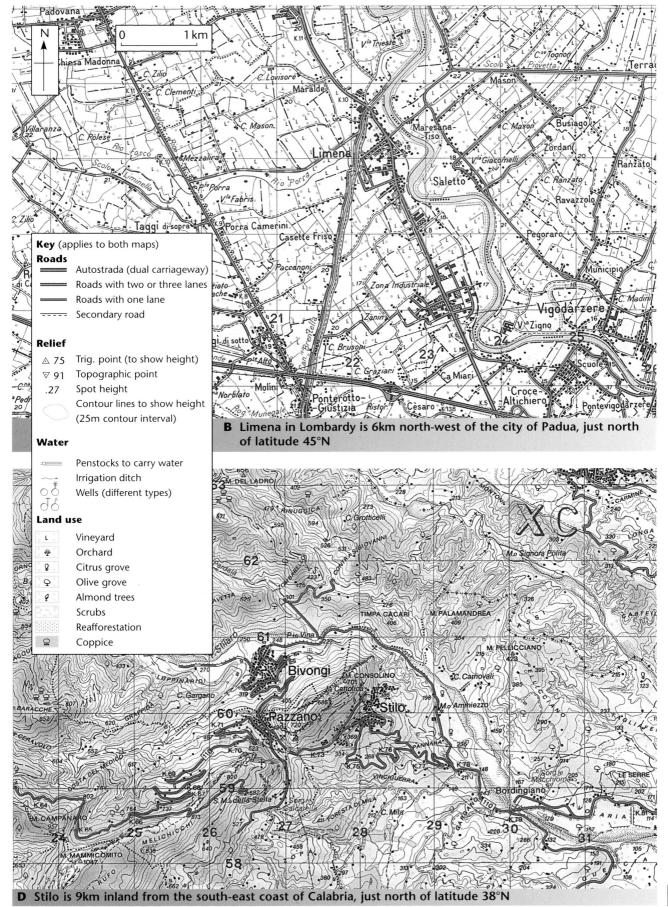

**Key** (applies to both maps)

**Roads**

▬▬▬ Autostrada (dual carriageway)

═══ Roads with two or three lanes

─── Roads with one lane

----- Secondary road

**Relief**

△ 75 Trig. point (to show height)

▽ 91 Topographic point

.27 Spot height

Contour lines to show height
(25m contour interval)

**Water**

Penstocks to carry water

Irrigation ditch

Wells (different types)

**Land use**

L Vineyard

Orchard

Citrus grove

Olive grove

Almond trees

Scrubs

Reafforestation

Coppice

**B** Limena in Lombardy is 6km north-west of the city of Padua, just north of latitude 45°N

**D** Stilo is 9km inland from the south-east coast of Calabria, just north of latitude 38°N

# Industry and services

> ▶ **What differences are there in manufacturing and service industries in different regions of Italy?**

## The multiplier effect in the North

About three-quarters of all jobs in manufacturing industry are in the northern regions of Italy. These are mostly in a triangle of industrial towns and cities that include Turin, Milan and Genoa.

Most of Italy's biggest manufacturing companies have their original factory and their headquarters in the north. These key industries

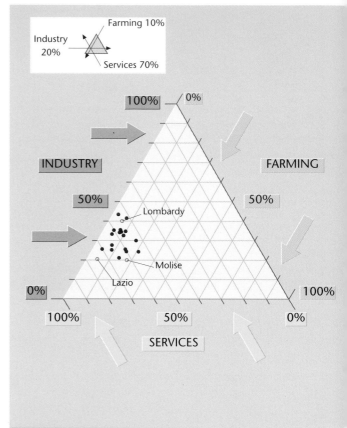

**B** Italy's employment structure

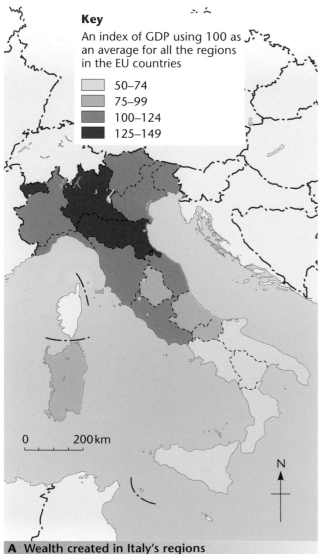

**Key**

An index of GDP using 100 as an average for all the regions in the EU countries

- 50–74
- 75–99
- 100–124
- 125–149

0    200 km

N

employ thousands of workers at their factories and in administration. The electronics company IBM, for example, employs 14 200 people in Lombardy. These industries have a **multiplier effect** on jobs by attracting smaller businesses. They also attract the whole range of services that people need in large built-up areas, such as shops, entertainment and public transport.

## A magnet for jobs

Jobs and working conditions in the largest companies and in **financial services**, such as banking, are often better paid than jobs in smaller companies. There is better training with better technology, so the workers are more highly skilled. A well-paid and skilled workforce helps attract even more businesses to the area.

**54** | **A** Wealth created in Italy's regions

The economic success of one region helps attract even more investment in new factories and services. A problem is that it holds back any other region from a share in new businesses and jobs.

## The centre and south

Many of the manufacturing industries in the centre and south are in small units that are sometimes run by a family. These industries are often in food processing and a range of **traditional craft** industries. There are some larger industries such as oil refining and making iron and steel. These, however, are the exception and have not attracted many other industries to locate near them.

## Single centres

The lack of industry in the south means there are no major **urban agglomerations** where towns and cities have joined together. Naples, Palermo and even smaller towns and cities have attracted some new jobs, but there is still a high rate of unemployment and poverty in these places. There are service jobs in tourism, in shops and in local government, but the better-paid jobs in banking and finance have also avoided locations in the south.

Rome is the main urban area away from the industrial cities of the north. Rome is big enough to have a good range of industries and services. Many of the service jobs are in tourism, government administration and retail trades.

## Contrasts within regions

Employment figures for provinces within each region often show wide differences in the kind of work that people do. In Piedmont, for example, 19 per cent of the workforce are in farming in the Asti district, while in Novara, only 3 per cent work in farming. In Turin, 45 per cent work in manufacturing compared with only 33 per cent in Alessandria. The percentage of workers in farming is even higher in some provinces in the south, and much lower for manufacturing industry.

**C** Packing dried figs in a food-processing factory near Naples

## FACT FILE

### Jobs in the region

The triangular graph B shows the different types of employment in the different regions of Italy. All the points on the graph cluster in one area of the graph. This means that the types of employment are similar in each region. There are between about 20 and 42 per cent of the people in each region working in industry. This may be in a big company such as FIAT or IBM, or in many smaller companies. There are between about 5 and 15 per cent working in farming, and in every region there are more than 50 per cent working in service jobs.

In every region, the type of work that people do has changed over the years. In most regions there are now fewer people working in manufacturing, and fewer in farming, but more in service jobs.

### Wealth in the regions

| % of total GDP | | | |
|---|---|---|---|
| Abruzzi | 1.9 | Marche | 2.6 |
| Apulia | 5.1 | Molise | 0.4 |
| Basilicata | 0.7 | Piedmont | 8.6 |
| Calabria | 2.2 | Sardinia | 2.2 |
| Campania | 6.9 | Sicily | 6.1 |
| Emilia-Romagna | 8.5 | Trentino-Alto Adige | 1.9 |
| Friuli-Venezia Giulia | 2.4 | Tuscany | 6.6 |
| Latium | 10.5 | Umbria | 1.3 |
| Liguria | 3.4 | Val d'Aosta | 0.3 |
| Lombardy | 19.5 | Veneto | 8.9 |

Wealth in the regions

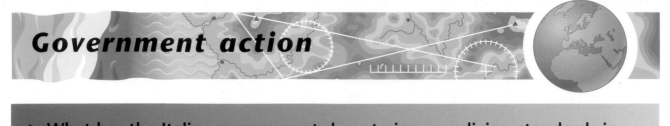

# Government action

▶ What has the Italian government done to improve living standards in the south?

▶ Have the government's plans worked?

## Making a start

In 1950, the Italian government began the job of improving people's standards of living in the south. One way to do this was to make sure there were more jobs in manufacturing industry and in the better-paid services.

The Italian government has tried to help the **Mezzogiorno** in different ways.
- Jobs in government departments were moved to new locations in the south.
- Some state-owned (nationalized) industries, such as steel-making, were moved to or set up in new sites in the south.
- Laws were changed to break up large farm estates so that more people could own their own land.
- New roads and other types of infrastructure such as power and water supplies were built with government money.
- New tax rules made it cheaper for new businesses to move to the south.
- Better ways of organizing the sale of farm produce were introduced.

## Organizing the changes

Between 1950 and 1984, improving the south was organized and paid for by a planning body named the Cassa per el Mezzogiorno. Money from the EEC (now the EU) was also used. Since then, improvement schemes have been continued by the Agency for the Promotion of the Development of the Mezzogiorno. The Istituto per la Ricostruzione Industriale (IRI) is another government organization that helps pay for new jobs and new roads. Mountain areas are given special help.

## New jobs

The plan at first was to concentrate new growth in a small number of places that planners call **growth poles**. The idea was that industries such as making cars and steel would help attract other businesses to the same area. These smaller businesses would make parts for cars or use steel to make other products.

Some of the new industries, such as making iron and steel at Taranto, were **labour intensive** industries that employed thousands of workers. Others, such as oil refineries, were **capital intensive** using automated methods and fewer workers.

## Limits to success

The effect of these plans has been that many new jobs have been created and more people now have a better standard of living. The plans, however, have not been completely successful. Some of the big factories have been left on their own in such a way that some people describe them as 'cathedrals in the desert'.

Another problem is that since the 1950s, the Italian government has sold most of its nationalized industries and does not subsidize

**A** An iron and steel works at Taranto in Apulia

**B** Heavy manufacturing industry helped by government and EU money at Porto Empedocle in south-west Italy

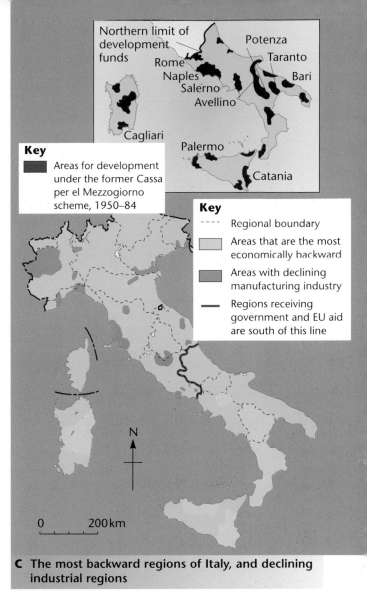

**Key**

▪ Areas for development under the former Cassa per el Mezzogiorno scheme, 1950–84

**Key**

- – – – Regional boundary
- ▢ Areas that are the most economically backward
- ▨ Areas with declining manufacturing industry
- ▬ Regions receiving government and EU aid are south of this line

**C** The most backward regions of Italy, and declining industrial regions

the new private companies. This makes it harder for the government to create jobs in regions that need help.

There are many new service jobs, especially in tourism. There are also some new businesses making foods, clothes and other goods. In spite of these changes, the problems of unemployment in the Mezzogiorno are far from over.

## FACT FILE

### A profile of Sicily

Sicily is one of the poorest regions in Italy, and in the European Union. It is the largest of Italy's regions in terms of size, and the third largest in population.

Most of Sicily is hilly or mountainous. There are some lowland plains near the coast, such as near Catania. In many places the rocks are chalk and limestone. These rocks break down to give thin, poor soils that do not hold water well. Mount Etna, on the eastern side of Sicily, is Europe's highest active volcano. It erupts regularly, sending streams of lava flowing down its slopes and covering the surrounding landscape with a coating of ash and dust.

People in Sicily make a living by farming, fishing, tourism, public services and in industries. Sicily is Italy's main region for producing citrus fruits such as lemons. Swordfish and tuna are traditional types of local fish. Industrial workers are employed in industries such as petrochemicals, engineering, pharmaceuticals and food processing.

Some of the jobs have been helped by money from the EU and from the Italian government. In spite of this, about one in five people in Sicily are still unemployed. Mafia crime is a problem, though many suspects have been arrested in recent years.

# The Emilia-Romagna region

▶ **What is the human and physical geography of the Emilia-Romagna region?**
▶ **How is the economy of the region changing?**
▶ **How does the changing economy affect people's lives and the environment?**

## Landscape and population

The Emilia-Romagna region is in the north of Italy. Part of the region is in the North Italian Plain, but further south the land rises to become part of the Apennine mountains. About 48 per cent of the region is plains with the rest either hills or mountains. The region has a coastline along the Adriatic Sea but it is shut off from the western coast by the Apennines.

There is no single **urban agglomeration** in the region. However, there is a line of towns and cities stretching from north to south along the route of an old Roman road. These include Bologna, Modena and Parma. There are also several cites and towns along the Adriatic coast. Some, such as Rimini, have become popular seaside holiday resorts.

Fewer people live in the hills and mountains. Many have left the more remote areas to go to live in the towns. In some, such as the mountain district of Piacenza, the population density is about half the average for Italy.

**B** Building Lamborghini cars at St Agata near Modena

## The region's economy

Just over one in ten of the workers are in farming, about one-third work in industry and the remainder work in service jobs. Jobs in farming have been falling, while jobs in the service industries have been increasing. The number of workers in manufacturing industry varies in different provinces from 27 to 44 per cent.

Some jobs are in traditional industries such as making clothes, food processing and ceramics. There are also modern high-tech jobs in electronics, building robots, and chemicals. The region's largest manufacturing industry is making agricultural machinery (by FIAT). Many of the region's products are exported both to other parts of Italy and to other countries. This has helped bring more money into the region and has helped create more jobs.

Another change is that there are now more women in paid employment. About 40 per cent of the workers are women. Many women work in the new service jobs such as in tourism, in shops and in banking and other financial services.

## Emilia-Romagna – the good life

Living in Emilia-Romagna has the advantage of good opportunities for work. So far, the region has avoided the problems that too much growth

**A** Emilia-Romagna

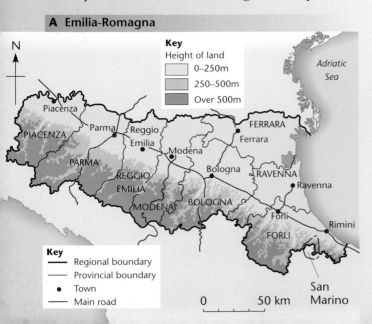

N

Key
Height of land
☐ 0–250m
☐ 250–500m
☐ Over 500m

Adriatic Sea

Piacenza
PIACENZA
Parma
PARMA
Reggio Emilia
REGGIO EMILIA
Modena
MODENA
FERRARA
Ferrara
Bologna
BOLOGNA
RAVENNA
Ravenna
Forli
FORLI
Rimini

Key
— Regional boundary
— Provincial boundary
● Town
— Main road

0     50 km

San Marino

can bring. Bologna, the largest city, still has a population of less than half a million people.

The surrounding countryside and coast include areas of attractive scenery. The new industries are mostly clean, although there are some environmental problems caused by sewage, chemicals from farms and from the rapid growth of tourism along the coast. Efforts are being made to ensure that the problems do not become serious, so that the region can continue to be an attractive place for people to work and live in.

**C  Looking over the streets of Bologna**

| Population and employment statistics for Emilia-Romagna | | | | | | |
|---|---|---|---|---|---|---|
| | Population (thousands) | Density per km² | %population change | % in agriculture | % in industry | % in services |
| Piacenza | 270 | 104 | −2.9 | 11 | 34 | 55 |
| Parma | 395 | 114 | −1.4 | 6 | 38 | 56 |
| Reggio Milia | 417 | 182 | 0.9 | 11 | 42 | 47 |
| Modena | 600 | 223 | 0.7 | 9 | 44 | 47 |
| Bologna | 912 | 246 | −2.0 | 6 | 35 | 59 |
| Ferrara | 366 | 139 | −3.8 | 14 | 32 | 54 |
| Ravenna | 352 | 189 | −1.9 | 16 | 27 | 57 |
| Forti | 601 | 201 | 1.7 | 11 | 29 | 60 |
| **Total** | **3925** | **177** | **−0.9** | **9** | **36** | **55** |

| Main employers in the Emilia-Romagna region | Total number of workers |
|---|---|
| State railways | 15 952 |
| Post and telecommunications | 5669 |
| FIAT farm machinery | 3192 |
| National telephone service | 2370 |
| Enichen Anic chemicals | 1512 |
| Weber car parts | 1458 |
| Enet | 1435 |

**D  Key economic statistics for Emilia-Romagna**

## FACT FILE

### Bologna profile

Bologna is the main city of the Emilia-Romagna region. It lies in a lowland area along the route of an old Roman road named the Via Amelia.

There are many historic buildings in Bologna including the cathedral of San Pietro (St Peter). The city claims to have Europe's oldest university. There is a medieval centre with arcades and shops. Bologna gives its name to the sauce that is often a part of Italian meat and pasta dishes – spaghetti bolognese, for example.

The city is now a manufacturing centre for farm machinery, food processing, chemicals, and a growing range of new high-tech and service industries.

### Ferrari's story

Ferrari cars are made by a company started in Emilia-Romagna by Enzo Ferrari, who lived between 1898 and 1988. He was a racing-car driver for a time, but in 1940 he began building his own cars, especially racing cars for Grand Prix races. Now the company also makes expensive sports cars.

The Ferrari car badge is a black horse on a yellow background. The horse was a symbol painted on the fuselage of an aircraft flown by the son of Count Enrico Baracca during the First World War. In 1923, the Count suggested to Enzo Ferrari that the symbol would bring him good luck. The colour yellow represents the city of Modena where Ferrari cars were made.

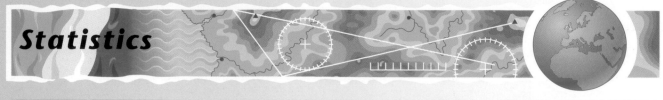

# Statistics

| | UK | ITALY | BRAZIL | JAPAN | INDIA |
|---|---|---|---|---|---|
| Total area (km²) | 244 100 | 301 270 | 8 511 965 | 377 801 | 3 287 260 |
| Total population (millions) | 58.3 | 57.2 | 159.1 | 125.2 | 943.0 |
| Population density: people per km² | 241 | 194 | 19 | 332 | 317 |

## Population

| | UK | ITALY | BRAZIL | JAPAN | INDIA |
|---|---|---|---|---|---|
| Birth rate per 1000 people | 14 | 11 | 26 | 10 | 31 |
| Death rate per 1000 people | 12 | 11 | 8 | 6 | 10 |
| Life expectancy (male and female) | 73M 79F | 73M 80F | 64M 69F | 76M 83F | 60M 61F |
| Fertility (children per female) | 2 | 1 | 3 | 2 | 4 |
| Population structure<br>0–14<br>15–59<br>60+ | 19%<br>60%<br>21% | 17%<br>63%<br>20% | 35%<br>58%<br>7% | 19%<br>64%<br>17% | 37%<br>56%<br>7% |
| Urban population | 89% | 67% | 76% | 77% | 26% |

## Environment and economy

| | UK | ITALY | BRAZIL | JAPAN | INDIA |
|---|---|---|---|---|---|
| Rate of urban growth per year | 0.3% | 0.6% | 2.3% | 0.6% | 2.9% |
| Land use: arable<br>grass<br>forest | 27%<br>46%<br>10% | 31%<br>17%<br>23% | 7%<br>22%<br>58% | 11%<br>2%<br>67% | 56%<br>4%<br>23% |
| % of workforce in: farming<br>industry<br>services | 2<br>28<br>70 | 9<br>32<br>59 | 25<br>25<br>50 | 7<br>34<br>59 | 62<br>11<br>27 |
| GNP per person (US$) | $17 970 | $19 620 | $2 920 | $31 450 | $290 |
| Unemployment | 9.4% | 11.6% | 5.9% | 3.0% | n/a |
| Energy used (tonnes/person/year) | 5.40 | 4.02 | 0.44 | 4.74 | 0.35 |

## Society and quality of life

| | UK | ITALY | BRAZIL | JAPAN | INDIA |
|---|---|---|---|---|---|
| Infant mortality (deaths per 1000 births) | 8 | 9 | 57 | 5 | 88 |
| People per doctor | 300 | 211 | 1000 | 600 | 2439 |
| Food supply (calories per person per day) | 3317 | 3561 | 2824 | 2903 | 2395 |
| Adult literacy | 99% | 97% | 81% | 99% | 50% |
| TVs per 1000 people | 434 | 421 | 207 | 613 | 35 |
| Aid received or given per person | $50 given | $53 given | $1.2 received | $90 given | $1.7 received |
| Education spending (% of GNP) | 5.3 | 4.1 | n/a | 5.0 | 3.5 |
| Military spending (% of GNP) | 4.0 | 2.0 | n/a | 1.0 | 2.5 |
| United Nations Human Development Index (out of 1.0) | 0.92 | 0.91 | 0.80 | 0.94 | 0.44 |

Figures are for 1992–95. Source: *Philip's Geographical Digest* (United Nations, World Bank). The Human Development Index is worked out by the UN. It is a summary of national income, life expectancy, adult literacy and education. It is a measure of human progress. In 1992, HDI ranged from 0.21 to 0.94.

# General

Longest river: River Po  (620km)
Highest mountain: Monte Rosa (4634m)
Largest lake: Lake Garda (370 km2)
Largest city: Rome (2.7 million)
Capital: Rome (2.7 million)
Languages: Italian (94%), Sardinian (3%)
Currency: Lira
Religion: Roman Catholic (83%)

## Population of largest cities

| | |
|---|---|
| Rome | 2 723 000 |
| Milan | 1 359 000 |
| Naples | 1 072 000 |
| Turin | 953 000 |
| Palermo | 697 000 |
| Genoa | 668 000 |

# Social

## Leisure (millions of lira spent)

| | |
|---|---|
| Theatres | 4.8 |
| Classical music (opera, ballet, concerts) | 4.3 |
| Light opera, musical comedy | 0.8 |
| Popular music (concerts, performances) | 2.8 |
| Cultural events | 0.1 |
| Cinema | 18.4 |
| Football | 8.8 |
| Other sporting events | 6.4 |
| Dance halls/musical events | 24.6 |
| Entertainment equipment/billiards/juke boxes | 10.5 |
| Other | 16.5 |

## Civil status of population (%)

| | Italy | UK* | USA |
|---|---|---|---|
| Single | 40.4 | 41.3 | 45.1 |
| Married | 48.5 | 45.6 | 44.3 |
| Divorced | 0.7 | 5.1 | 6.7 |
| Widowed | 5.2 | 7.0 | 5.1 |

*estimate only

## Crime (per 100 000 people)

| | Italy | UK | USA | Australia |
|---|---|---|---|---|
| Murder | 14.4 | 2.5 | 9.3 | 1.9 |
| Theft | 2 931* | 8 135 | 4 903 | 5 885 |

[* UBIS checking]

# Economic

## Imports  and exports (%)

| | Imports | Exports |
|---|---|---|
| Food and live animals | 10.7 | 5.4 |
| Beverages and tobacco | 1.1 | 1.2 |
| Crude materials (excluding fuels) | 6.4 | 1.0 |
| Mineral fuels, lubricants | 8.5 | 2.0 |
| Animal and vegetable oils and fats | 0.6 | 0.4 |
| Chemicals | 11.3 | 6.9 |
| Manufactured goods | 24.9 | 45.2 |
| Machinery and transport equipment | 31.9 | 36.8 |
| Miscellaneous goods | 4.7 | 1.1 |
| Total (US $ million) | 188 706 | 170 402 |

## Agricultural land usage

| | |
|---|---|
| Area (1000ha) | 17 597 |
| % of total area | 58.4 |
| Arable land | 8 958 |
| Crops (% of arable land): | |
| cereals | 51.8 |
| potatoes | 1.5 |
| sugar beet | 3.4 |
| oilseed rape | 0.3 |
| sunflowers | 1.2 |
| permanent crops | 17.1 |
| permanent grass | 27.6 |
| Woods (% of total area) | 30.2 |
| Animals (000s) | |
| cattle | 8 235 |
| pigs | 8 837 |
| sheep | 10 848 |
| Farms | 2 774 |
| Average size (ha) | 6.3 |

## Tourism (1993)

| | Italy | UK | USA |
|---|---|---|---|
| Foreign tourists | 26 379 000 | 19 488 000 | 45 779 000 |
| Amount spent (US $) | 20 521 000 | 13 451 000 | 57 621 000 |

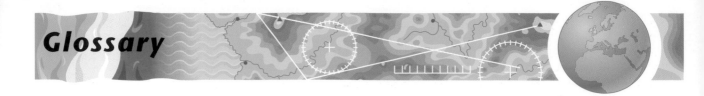

**active** a volcano that constantly or regularly erupts

**administrative regions** areas defined for administrative reasons inside a country

**age–sex pyramid** (*see* population pyramid)

**alternative energy** types of energy that are natural and that do not use fossil fuels

**altitude** the height of land above sea level

**avalanche** a rapid fall of mud, rock, snow or ice down a slope

**balance of payments** the difference between the value of imports and exports

**birth rate** the number of children born for every 1000 people in a year

**bora** a cold wind that blows south over the Adriatic Sea

**calderas** the remains of very large volcanic craters

**capital intensive** using money to buy machinery and other technology instead of using people to do the work

**catchment area** the area drained by a river system

**city state** a small country that consists of one city and its surrounding countryside

**commercial** run as a profit-making business

**coniferous trees** trees that have needle-leaves and cones

**conserve** to manage and protect for the future

**container port** a port with special facilities to handle freight containers

**crust** the hard outer layer of the Earth

**death rate** the number of deaths for every 1000 people in a year

**deciduous trees** trees that mostly shed their leaves

**degradation** where the soil becomes useless for farming

**deltas** natural features built up where a river deposits its load at its mouth or in other places where its flow is suddenly slowed down

**demographic transition** the way that a country's birth rate, death rate and population total change over time

**dependency load** the ratio of people in work to those who are not

**depressions** moving areas of low pressure, often with strong winds and rain

**desertification** a soil is changed to desert conditions, with very little water

**discharge** the amount of water flowing past a point in a river, measured in cubic metres per second (cumecs)

**dormant** a volcano that has not erupted for several hundred years, but may erupt in the future

**drought** a period of several months when there is no rain

**economically developed country** (**EDC**) country that has a high level of GNP per capita (per person)

**economically less developed country** country that has a low GNP per capita

**economy** the way a country creates its wealth

**ecosystem** a set of links between vegetation, climate and other parts of the environment

**emigration** to leave one country to go and live in another country

**European Union** the group of 15 countries that work together to improve their trade, economic, social and environmental policies

**exports** goods sold to another country

**extensive** using a large amount of land in a way that produces a low yield per hectare

**extinct** a volcano that will never erupt again

**false colours** colours used on satellite images that are unlike real colours on the ground

**fault lines** breaks through layers of rock

**fertility rate** the number of children born to each woman

**financial services** businesses that handle money, such as banking and insurance

**finite resources** resources that will run out

**flash floods** floods that happen very quickly

**focus** the point underground where rocks move and cause an earthquake

**folded** layers of rock that have been pushed together and shaped into folds

**fossil fuels** sources of energy formed from ancient vegetation or animal life

**fronts** boundary lines between different types of air, such as between warm air and cold air

**fumaroles** holes through which steam and gases from volcanic rocks come to the surface

**garrigue** a type of scrubland in very dry areas

**geographic information system** (**GIS**) using maps and data to solve location problems

**geothermal** heat from below the ground

**glaciers** ice masses in a valley

**global warming** a slow rise in temperature over the Earth

**gross domestic product** (**GDP**) the wealth created in a country

**gross national product** (**GNP**) a measure of the wealth created by a country's businesses both at home and abroad

**growth poles** areas chosen to be centres for new economic growth

**gully erosion** narrow deep cuts into a slope where soil has been washed away

**habitat** an environment that is home for animals

**'hidden economy'** sometimes referred to as the 'black economy': unofficial ways that people earn money and do not pay taxes

**high pressure area** an area where a large body of air is sinking

**human geography** the study of how people interact with their environment

**humus** rotting vegetation in a soil

**hydroelectric** electricity produced by using the force of falling water

**immigrants** people who come into a country from another country

**impermeable** will not let water pass through it

**imports** goods bought from another country

**infinite** will never run out

**infrastructure** provision of basic services such as water, electricity, roads, communications

**inputs** something that goes into a system

**intensive** done with great attention to getting the maximum output

**irrigated** to carry water onto fields for farming

**joint ventures** done by agreement between two or more companies, sometimes in different countries

**labour intensive** making use of people instead of machinery

**lagoon** an area of calm, shallow water cut off from the sea by a sand or gravel bank

**landslide** where soil and rock collapse down a slope

**lava** molten rock that flows from a volcano or from fissures (cracks) in the Earth's surface

**licence** a legal agreement that gives permission

**life expectancy** how long a person can expect to live

**liquefaction** when soil is shaken loose by an earthquake

**magma** molten material from under the Earth's crust

**magma chambers** underground reservoirs of magma for a volcano

**manufacturing industry** making goods in factories

**maquis** a type of scrubland in dry areas

**meanders** bends in a river's course

**Mediterranean climate** a type of climate over the Mediterranean Sea and surrounding land, as well as in other places in similar locations

**metamorphic** a type of rock that has been formed by great pressure and heat

**Mezzogiorno** ('land of the midday sun') the name given to the regions in the south of Italy

**migration** movement from one place to another

**mistral** a cold wind that blows south down the Rhône valley

**monarchy** a country that has a king or queen

**multiplier effect** how one development leads to another

**natural disasters** loss of life and property due to an act of nature

**natural increase** the annual increase in a country's population

**natural vegetation** the type of vegetation that would grow naturally in an area

**network** a set of links

**newly industrialized countries (NICs)** countries that have rapidly increased their GNP by developing more industry

**overgrazing** too many animals removing vegetation and exposing soil

**peninsula** an area of land that juts out into the sea

**per capita** for each person

**permanent cultivation** land that is always being farmed

**physical geography** the study of how natural processes affect the landscape

**plate** a large section of the Earth's crust

**population density** the number of people living in an area, for example in one square kilometre

**population distribution** the pattern of where people live

**population pyramid** a graph showing the percentage of people of different ages and genders in a country

**population structure** the proportion of people of different ages and genders

**precipitation** rain, snow and other forms of water from the sky

**provinces** sub-divisions of an administrative region

**quota** an amount or number that is allowed

**raw materials** the original materials that are needed to make manufactured products

**reclaiming** making land that was once unusable into useful land

**regime** the pattern of a river's flow throughout the year

**remote sensing** collecting data from sensors on satellites

**Renaissance** a period of new ideas in art, thinking and science between the thirteenth and seventeenth centuries

**renewable** resources that can be replaced

**republic** a country without a king or queen

**resources** things that can be used

**rural areas** countryside areas

**rural depopulation** people leaving the countryside

**satellite image** a picture created from electronic data collected by sensors on satellites

**screes** piles of weathered rock that falls to the bottom of a slope

**scrubland** areas with little vegetation except low grass and bushes

**seasonal** at certain times of the year

**sheet erosion** where a slope is stripped bare of its soil

**shock waves** ripples of energy from an earthquake

**silt** fine mud carried in a river

**sirocco** a warm wind that blows north from North Africa

**site** the land on which something is built

**slope failure** when the natural angle of rest of a slope is changed and there is a landslide

**soil erosion** soil that is washed or blown away

**solar power** to capture and use energy from the sun

**storm hydrograph** a graph that shows how a river behaves after a rainstorm

**subsidence** ground that sinks or collapses

**subsidies** money paid to help keep a business running

**surface runoff** rainwater that flows off the land's surface

**sustained** can carry on at the same level in the future

**tap roots** long roots that reach down to underground water

**terraces** steps cut into a hillside for farming

**tidal range** the difference in height between high tide and low tide

**trade** to buy and sell goods between countries

**traditional craft** an old way of making something

**transpiration** moisture that comes off leaves

**tributaries** smaller rivers that join larger rivers

**tsunami** a giant wave caused by an earthquake or volcanic eruption

**urban agglomerations** large built-up areas

**urban areas** towns and cities

**weathered** broken down by the weather

**wind turbines** turbines that use the wind to generate electricity

**yields** the amount of produce from a crop

**zero population growth** when the population of a country does not change year after year

# Index

Bold type refers to terms included in the glossary

*Italic* type refers to photographs or maps